THE SILVER GRINGO

the
SILVER
GRINGO

WILLIAM SPRATLING AND TAXCO

Joan Mark

UNIVERSITY OF NEW MEXICO PRESS ✳ ALBUQUERQUE

Library of Congress

Cataloging-in-Publication Data

Mark, Joan T.

The silver gringo:

William Spratling and Taxco

Joan Mark. – 1st ed.

p. cm.

Includes bibliographical references (p. 141) and index.

ISBN 0-8263-2079-1 (cloth:alk. paper)

1. Spratling, William, 1900–1967—Criticism and interpretation.

2. Silverwork—Mexico—Taxco de Alarcon—History—20th century.

3. Silversmiths—Mexico—Taxco de Alarcon.

I. Title.

NK7198.S67 M37 2000

739.2372—dc21

99-6395

CIP

Designed by Sue Niewiarowski

Frontispiece: William Spratling, 1963.
Photo courtesy of Mary Anita Loos von Saltza.

Contents

INTRODUCTION

Bill Spratling was tall, thin, almost gaunt, but handsome in a rugged way, with dark hair, a long nose, an angular jaw, and a carefully trimmed mustache. He wore thick dark-rimmed glasses. His voice was deep with an Alabama drawl that could pull a simple name out to four syllables. "He called me 'C*a*-a-r-l'," the artist Carl Pappé remembered. "He had a voice just like William Faulkner's."

The deep voice and the drawl were those of his father, born on an Alabama plantation. But the southern drawl had been reinforced in New Orleans through his friendship with Bill Faulkner. Already that was becoming a useful name to drop, at least with those few of his countrymen he happened to encounter in Mexico.

He first went to Mexico in the summer of 1926, when he was twenty-six years old. He immediately made friends, as he nearly always managed to do, with the most interesting people around. In Mexico City he met the painter Diego Rivera and a high-spirited young Mexican government official named Moisés Sáenz and the anthropologist Manuel Gamio. He sent an article about them to *Scribner's Magazine.* "Figures in a Mexican Renaissance," he called it. Mexico was emerging from a decade of revolution, and they were the advance guard, unknown as yet in the United States. He began to think of himself as their North American publicist.

But it was the land outside of Mexico City that captured his imagination—the dramatic changes of climate as he moved from Mexico City up through pine forests and then down to the year-around spring of Cuernavaca or east to the tropical coast of Veracruz or south to the mountains of Guerrero. "This strange countryside," he called it, with its "rich" and "savage" beauty and the "unending rhythm of the eternal mountains."[1] He liked the harshness of Mexico, the cruelty of the barren mountains, the sweat of the tropics, the acrid smells, the smoke from charcoal fires, the burning taste of tequila. Surely the geography of this place has shaped its human inhabitants, he thought. From it the Indians took their strong sense of form and color and the vigor of their art. From it the Spanish took an exhilaration and a zeal for building. He felt that exhilaration himself.

2   It was the Spanish buildings that had brought him to Mexico. He had a commission from *Architectural Forum* to do some articles on Mexican colonial architecture and illustrate them with his own sketches. So he spent the summer traveling and sketching—cathedrals, palaces, abandoned monasteries. He went to Cuernavaca where Cortés had had a palace; to Puebla with its 365 churches, one for every day of the year; to Taxco, the old mining town hidden off in the Sierra Madre south of Mexico City.

The rough, winding road over the mountains to Taxco was breathtaking, until night suddenly fell. He made his way into the town in the dark. When he stepped out of his small posada the next morning, he found himself looking down on a white cloud bank that covered the entire lower half of the town. Far off to the south and the west a few mountain tops loomed up, "like blue islands in a white sea."[2] Taxco was on a mountain slope so steep that the highest parts of the town were six hundred feet above the lowest parts. It was a town of three dimensions, instead of the two that he had grown accustomed to in the flat delta of New Orleans. Later, as he walked the narrow cobblestone streets lined with whitewashed houses and mule trains bringing in supplies, he felt as if he had suddenly been transported to provincial Spain in the mid-seventeenth century.

It was obvious that from its beginnings this town had experienced the swift shifts in fortune that go with mining. Taxco has two landmarks dating from the two prosperous periods in its history. An aqueduct with large arches at the north end of town had been part of a silver compound that belonged to Hernán Cortés. The Spanish found silver here in 1534. Within forty years they had transformed the barren mountainside with a few cactuses and a small settlement of Chontal Indians into a town of silver haciendas and Franciscan monasteries, where merchants ate from silver dishes and church officials wore silks and brocades. But then the boom had ended.

The second landmark is a jewel of colonial architecture, the parish church of Santa Prisca, which dominates the central plaza. It was built by a Spanish miner who had found a rich vein of silver in the nearby La Lajuela mine in 1748. José de la Borda paid for the church of carved pink stone with a glowing tiled dome and nine gilded altarpieces inside. Borda built himself an elegant home nearby, on an adjacent side of the town plaza. He was the town patron, paving roads, piping in water, setting up fountains and public laundry tubs, roofing the homes of the poor. Then the silver gave out, and Borda left town to try his hand elsewhere. For the second time in its history, Taxco settled back into being an impoverished old mining town, down on its luck, but with the memory, made visible in these two landmarks, of having twice been brought to greatness and wealth by energetic outsiders.

It would happen again. Of course, in 1926, Bill Spratling did not know that. All he knew was that he loved Mexico and wanted to return. The land suited him because it mirrored him. It was harsh, tough, and weighted with secret sorrows.

Three years later, when he needed a refuge, he came back.

CHAPTER ONE

The Road to Mexico

The road to Mexico ran south, from upstate New York to Baltimore, to Atlanta, to Auburn, Alabama, and then to New Orleans.

William P. Spratling, Jr., was born on September 22, 1900, in Sonyea, in upstate New York, where his physician father, Dr. William P. Spratling, Sr., was medical superintendent at the Craig Colony, a model state sanitarium for epileptics. Spratling's mother, Anna Gorton, was a New Englander from a prominent family in Rhode Island. Bill was the second of three children, with an older sister, Lucille, and a younger brother, David. In 1908 the family moved to Baltimore, Maryland, where Dr. Spratling became professor of physiology and diseases of the nervous system at the College of Physicians and Surgeons.

This seemingly secure and upper-middle-class world was shattered in 1911 when Dr. Spratling suffered a severe nervous breakdown. He left his family and retired to Welaka, Florida, where he put himself under the care of a physician friend. There he died in 1915, at the age of fifty-three, in a hunting accident that may have been a suicide. An obituary in the *Journal of Nervous and Mental Diseases* at the time described him as a kindly and much-loved man whose former patients sought him out in Florida and who shared his knowledge and love of the outdoors with a crowd of boys who gathered around him.[1] But his own two sons were hundreds of miles away.

In Baltimore, Anna Gorton Spratling struggled to keep her family together, even, as Spratling would later note bitterly, taking in sewing for her wealthy friends. Then she died, in 1912. The children were separated and farmed out to relatives. Bill spent a summer on his grandfather Spratling's plantation in Alabama and then two years with an unsympathetic uncle in Atlanta. When he was fourteen, he was sent to stay with a cousin, Mrs. Leila Avery Terrell, a young widow with three small children who ran a boardinghouse in Auburn, Alabama, for students at Auburn University.

Auburn, Alabama, was a small, football-obsessed college town in the Deep South. It was not a particularly congenial place for a shy and sensitive young man who wanted to be an artist, but Bill Spratling made his peace with it. He waited on tables at the boardinghouse to earn his keep while he finished high school. Then he attended the local university. He liked to draw, so he earned his spending money doing banners for football games, the art work in the college annual, the Gothic script on the college diplomas. At the university he was a prodigy, doing so well in his architecture courses that from his sophomore year on he was hired to teach some of them. He taught descriptive geometry, anatomy (using a book of drawings), the history of architecture (using slides from the school library), and even topographical map-making for the military. As with many young architects, the principles of architecture and design became for him "a sort of religion." It was his way of bringing order to a chaotic world. But his difficult childhood had left scars. He described himself as "an inhibited, shy, frequently depressed boy."[2] He would always be an intensely private man. His brother-in-law, Dr. Edward Bleier, once described the three Spratling siblings as being very different one from the other but united in their aversion to having any questions asked about their private affairs.[3]

Spratling left Auburn without a degree in 1921 (he lacked a few credits in mathematics) and took a job as draftsman with an architectural firm in Birmingham. A year later he went to New Orleans as adjunct professor in the School of Architecture at Tulane University and moved into the French Quarter.

The French Quarter in the early 1920s was an area of decaying but interesting old buildings with a bohemian writer's colony presided over by Sherwood Anderson and Lyle Saxon. Spratling rented an apartment from Natalie Scott, the society editor for one of the local newspapers, at 624 Orleans's Alley (later called Pirate's Alley) near the St. Louis cathedral. There he gave parties several nights a week, dispensing hospitality "with an easy efficiency that puts many hostesses to shame," according to Natalie Scott.[4] He served absinthe, which he bought in great jugs from the widow of a bootlegger, or gin made from gallons of alcohol and bottled juniper berry essence aerated by rolling the barrels on the attic floor. Bill Spratling's studio was "our main gathering place," Oliver La Farge wrote later, reminiscing about his years in New Orleans.[5]

Spratling escaped the summer heat in New Orleans by taking a freighter to Europe. In 1923 he traveled in France. In 1924 he went to Italy, Egypt, and Greece. He returned home with treasures, including Oriental rugs, and boasted that the entire trip, with rugs, had cost him only $325. And the parties continued. A local paper described one gathering at Spratling's as "a steady flow of conversation,

William Spratling, "Orleans Alley." The Historic New Orleans Collection.

William Spratling, "Docks,"
c. 1925. The Historic
New Orleans Collection.

unstudied and amusing," stimulated by the room itself which was a "pleasant harmony of things chosen with discriminating taste . . . a cloth in Egyptian design over the mantel, a weaving on the wall, elsewhere a Paisley, a Piranesi, a sketch of Venice done by the host." Presiding over it all was Spratling himself with a "twinkling sidewise turn" in his large brown eyes and a "slow, quiet chuckling ripple of a laugh."[6]

In 1925 William Faulkner turned up in New Orleans, and for four months he and a young newspaperman named Louis Piper lived in two rooms on the ground floor of Spratling's apartment, while Spratling lived on the second floor. Spratling gave them breakfast, let them use his bathroom, and had Leonore, the black woman who cooked for him, clean up after them. Faulkner wrote his mother that it was "the best spot in New Orleans in which to live."[7]

Faulkner was twenty-seven, two years older than Spratling, and known primarily at that time as a poet. He and Spratling became "drinking and carousing partners,"[8] but more than that, they were two very talented young men, each with a touch of genius, playing their creativity off each other.

Both of them worked very hard in New Orleans. Faulkner was up early every morning, sometimes as early as four A.M., typing on the balcony with a drink already at hand, as Spratling described him,[9] working on his first novel, *Soldier's Pay,* and gathering material for his second, *Mosquitoes.* Spratling turns up repeatedly, in a disguised form, in both of these early Faulkner novels. He recognized himself in *Soldier's Pay* in Private Joe Gilligan's gruff exterior and authoritarian way of taking care of people. In *Mosquitoes,* a fictionalized version of a boating party on Lake Pontchartrain presided over by Sherwood Anderson, some of Spratling's qualities are given to the sculptor Gordon and others to the silent poet Mark Frost. Gordon's attic studio is Spratling's. Frost, invited up to a woman's apartment late at night, lies on the sofa smoking cigarette after cigarette, while his negligee-clad hostess waits in vain for him in the bedroom. In *Mosquitoes* Faulkner also used a story Spratling liked to tell, from his summer on his grandfather's plantation, about a young boy and a girl peering upside down at one another in a primitive outhouse. In the novel Faulkner gives the story to the voluble Sherwood Anderson character rather than to either of the Spratling-like characters.[10]

But it is in one of the nonfiction sketches about New Orleans people that Faulkner wrote for the *Times-Picayune,* a local newspaper, that their friendship is most truly revealed. "Out of Nazareth," as the essay is called, begins with Faulkner and Spratling strolling through Jackson Park, admiring the green trees and grass, the hyacinths and narcissi. Faulkner wrote, "I remarked to Spratling how no one since Cézanne had really dipped his brush in light. Spratling, whose hand has been shaped to a brush as mine has (alas!) not, here became discursive on the subject of transferring light to canvas."[11]

They walked on. "And then . . . ," Faulkner wrote, "we saw him. . . . Spratling saw him first. 'My God,' he said, clutching me, 'look at that face.'"

A young man was staring up at the cathedral, with a small pack and a staff at his side. Faulkner wrote:

And one could imagine young David looking like that. One could imagine Jonathan getting that look from David, and, serving the highest function of which sorry man is capable, being the two of them beautiful in similar peace and simplicity—beautiful as gods, as no woman can ever be. And to think of speaking to him, of entering that dream, was like a desecration.

William Spratling, "St. Louis Cathedral," 1923. The Historic New Orleans Collection.

But they did speak to him. They took the young man to lunch at Victor's and learned that he was seventeen years old, a farm boy from the Middle West, a would-be writer on the road who lived by picking up odd jobs.

11

Later, back on the street and ready to part, they offered him money, but the boy refused it. Spratling asked him to come and model for him the next afternoon, but the boy did not want to commit himself. Finally, he accepted a dollar on the condition that Faulkner, a fellow writer, take in return an essay he had written about his life on the road. Faulkner reproduced the essay and commented, "Some of the words mean nothing, as far as I know (and words are my meat and bread and drink), but to change them would be to destroy David himself." He ended with the boy's explanation: " 'You see,' he told us, 'I can always write another one.' "

In this bold piece Faulkner casually acknowledges Spratling's interest in young men and more grudgingly acknowledges his talent as an artist ("whose hand has been shaped to a brush as mine has [alas!] not"). The essay begins with Spratling, with his talent and his sensitivity to the colors of nature, to the beauty of the boy, and to the beauty of the cathedral the boy is admiring. It jumps with an interior monologue from the boy admiring the church to two boys admiring one another, to the biblical friends, David and Jonathan, "beautiful as gods—as no woman could ever be." Then, however, they discover that the young farm boy is a would-be writer, and Faulkner, the writer, becomes the true subject of the rest of the story. "Words are my meat and bread and drink," he says of himself, and the young boy's confidence and productivity ("I can always write another one") are his own.

Spratling also was extremely productive in New Orleans. He drew constantly, and he exhibited his work, portfolios of New Orleans, sketches of Florence, Venice, Genoa, and Rome, and an occasional nude, in annual shows at the local Arts and Crafts Club. Alongside his teaching at Tulane, he started an evening school for young men from the local engineering and architectural offices. He taught them free-hand drawing, descriptive geometry, shadow perspective, and the history of architecture, and he wrote a small manual, *Pencil Drawing*, expressly for them.

Spratling was as lyrical about a simple tool, the pencil, as he would later be about a modest metal, silver. A lead pencil, he wrote, is

> the ideal medium, extending from an instrument of extreme delicacy and precision, yielding a silvery lustrous line, to the thick soft lead possessing the rich blackness of charcoal, though retaining its own metallic lustre.[12]

The pencil "becomes a magic wand in his trained fingers," one critic wrote.[13] Another marveled at how with only a pencil he could produce lines as soft and broad as the strokes of a brush or as fine as the point of an etcher's needle.[14]

William Spratling, "Belle Alliance Plantation," c. 1925. The Historic New Orleans Collection.

Spratling was equally skilled at design and composition. He liked bird's-eye views from unexpected angles. He easily grasped and could render architectural forms in rhythmic lines and patterns, at the same time suggesting space and distance.

Surrounded as he was by writers in New Orleans, Spratling too began producing books. The manual on drawing, *Pencil Drawing,* was illustrated with small sketches he had made in France. He and Lyle Saxon did a book together entitled *Picturesque New Orleans,* with a text by Saxon and illustrations by Spratling. He and Natalie Scott traveled the bayous of the state together for the book *Plantation Houses of Louisiana.* Spratling sketched the buildings while Natalie Scott talked to the inhabitants, and she finally wrote the text, but it took her three years to do so, to Spratling's frustration. It would have been easier to have done it all himself. He described himself in these years as "primarily an artist, though by trade an architect and inclination a story-teller."[15]

In the summer of 1925 Spratling again went to Europe on a freighter, this time to do some essays on Italy for *Architectural Forum*. At the last minute Faulkner decided to go with him. In Europe they traveled together briefly, then split up. Spratling returned to New Orleans for the fall term at Tulane. Faulkner stayed on in Europe and then in February of 1926 returned to New Orleans and again moved in with Spratling. The latter had moved across the block from his old apartment to a fourth-floor attic at 632 St. Peter Street (the sculptor's studio in *Mosquitoes*). Faulkner helped him build a deck on the steep roof from which they could look down over the street and the rooftops of the French Quarter. At least one of their antics, aiming a BB gun at the girls in the ballet school across the street, is still remembered in New Orleans today.[16]

In the summer of 1926 Spratling made his first trip to Mexico. Franz Blom who taught archaeology at Tulane had given him an introductory letter to Diego Rivera. Through Diego he met a group of artists and intellectuals in Mexico City including twenty-three-year-old Miguel Covarrubias, whose caricatures of prominent New Yorkers, *The Prince of Wales and Other Famous Americans*, had been a best-seller in the United States the year before. Covarrubias was "dashing and brilliant,"[17] Spratling wrote Natalie Scott, and just back from New York, where his latest exhibit, on Harlem, had been a sensation.

In New Orleans that fall, Spratling tried his own hand at caricatures of his friends in the French Quarter. He called it *Sherwood Anderson and Other Famous Creoles,* and dedicated it "with Respectful Deference to Miguel Covarrubias" as well as "To All the Artful and Crafty Ones of the French Quarter." Spratling's drawings were satirical but affectionate. Like Covarrubias's, they were not so much caricatures as a subtle form of social observation. One was of himself and Faulkner (who was named co-author) at work with a bottle of moonshine under the table. Another had Sherwood Anderson sunk deep in a low chair wearing loud plaid pants and spats. Faulkner wrote the introduction to the book, just four paragraphs, in a style that mimicked Sherwood Anderson's. That too was intended to be a light-hearted spoof. But the joke turned sour, for Sherwood Anderson and his wife Elizabeth, who had befriended Faulkner and Spratling, rather resented it.

At this point the New Orleans scene began to sour. Sherwood and Elizabeth Anderson left in the fall of 1926, going to a farm in Virginia where they built a stone house according to designs Spratling sent them. Anderson later rather downplayed Spratling's contribution, writing that "we could not use the plans much, as neither the builder Ball or myself could understand the blueprints."[18] Faulkner went back to his home in Mississippi. Oliver La Farge would soon leave. Spratling continued to teach at Tulane, but he spent summers in Mexico, returning in 1927 and 1928 to teach courses on Spanish colonial architecture in a summer

William Spratling and William Faulkner, *Sherwood Anderson and Other Famous Creoles*, 1926.

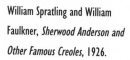

school for foreigners (mostly teachers of Spanish from Texas and California) at Mexican National University.

Around the time Faulkner left New Orleans, Spratling began to write short word portraits of people similar to those Faulkner had done for the *Times-Picayune*. *Scribner's Magazine* in 1928 published "Cane River Portraits" by William Spratling, five drawings of people he found living along the Cane River three hundred miles north of New Orleans, accompanied by brief descriptions of the people, their reactions to being drawn, and their world of impoverished cotton plantations and fading French traditions. A remarkable amount of history and psychological understanding is conveyed in just eight pages.

Then Spratling turned to his new friends in Mexico. He did sketches, in words and pen, of Diego Rivera, Moisés Sáenz (the undersecretary of public education who had hired him to teach in the summer school), the artist and volcano expert Dr. Atl, the anthropologist Manuel Gamio, and others, calling them "Figures in a

Mexican Renaissance," which *Scribner's* also published. The sketches are superb, the word portraits less satisfactory. Spratling was too much a propagandist for the new world he had just discovered and too aware that his subjects were likely to read what he had written about them to analyze them acutely. But he would use the same form—pen sketches and word portraits—again and brilliantly in a future book about Mexico.

In 1929 Spratling decided to move permanently to Taxco. The reason for the move is unclear. In *File on Spratling,* an autobiographical memoir he dictated shortly before his death, he said simply that after three summers in Mexico, he was caught up in the rhythm of life there and that he had a contract from a New York publisher for a book on Mexico which gave him a reason to leave Tulane. In fact, however, by the fall of 1928, he had already left Tulane and was sharing Lyle Saxon's apartment on Christopher Street in Greenwich Village with Bill Faulkner.[19] Spratling spent several months in New York, doing sketches for theater programs and making contacts with literary people. He also tried to help his Mexican friends, particularly Diego Rivera who at that time was almost unknown in the United States. He persuaded the Museum of Modern Art to give Diego Rivera his first show in New York, and he persuaded the Fine Arts Committee of the Architects Institute of America to give Diego Rivera their Gold Medal.

In Lyle Saxon's papers there is a letter from a friend, Joe, who also lived in Saxon's apartment, reporting on Spratling's activities in New York in February of 1929. He wrote:

> Bill is well . . . again . . . and very much in love with someone that is
> not in love with him, nor ever will be. That's good for him. He's going to
> Mexico in March to be assistant director for some movie a society dame is
> sponsoring. Sounds like a waste of time to me but all expenses paid. As for
> his career in New York, he's killing it off by degrees. He's so busy reaching
> for the next rung in the ladder he's going to miss it *and* the one he's
> standing on and fall through.[20]

The movie may have been Sergei Eisenstein's unfinished epic on Mexico which was financed by Mary Craig Sinclair, the wealthy wife of Upton Sinclair. If that was the arrangement, it fell apart. Eisenstein did not arrive in Mexico to make the movie until 1930. By then Spratling had been in Mexico for a year and had settled into his writing career in Taxco.

One story told in Taxco is that Spratling came to Mexico to recover from a nervous breakdown. The comment "Bill is well again" may refer to this. Another persistent rumor in Mexico holds that it was a homosexual incident, possibly one involving a student, that caused Spratling's departure from Tulane.[21] That this or something similar may have at least caused difficulties for him is hinted at by Spratling himself in a book review he sent back to the *New York Herald Tribune* shortly after his arrival in Mexico.

In New York Spratling had met Irita Van Doren, editor of the book section of the Sunday *New York Herald Tribune,* and offered to send her literary news columns and book reviews from Mexico. She would publish at least a dozen such short essays by him over the next three years, part of an effort to expand the international coverage of the book section. Spratling's first "Mexican Letter" appeared on March 24, 1929. Six weeks later, on June 2, 1929, he reviewed a French novel about lesbianism, *Marie Bonifas* by Jacques de Lacretelle. In his review, Spratling stressed the innocence of homosexual love. It may be "unnatural," he wrote, but it is innocent and chaste and remains so, through "the inevitable accusations of depraved sensuality." He praised the author Lacretelle's "delicacy and deep pity" in writing about the subject with such care that "one never has the feeling of peering in upon unspeakable privacies." Spratling compared *Marie Bonifas* with Radclyffe Hall's well-known lesbian novel, *The Well of Loneliness,* and summarized their two theories about sexual aberration. Radclyffe Hall thought that one is born an "invert," a member of the "third sex," while Lacretelle believed "that sexual aberration results from faulty training during infancy and childhood, that it is inborn but due to unusual environmental circumstances." Spratling added, "The truth of the matter is that present-day science recognizes elements of validity in both positions."[22]

Spratling's review of *Marie Bonifas* was an indirect but bold assertion of who he was and who he intended to keep on being, despite "the inevitable accusations of depraved sensuality." He had not reviewed books before and would seldom do so again. But singling out this particular novel to review allowed him to make public his views on homosexual acts, to answer his critics, to justify, or at least exonerate, himself. Spratling lived by a strong personal code of honor, a gentleman's code, to which he adhered all his life. It had to do with paying his debts, keeping his word, treating his fellow human beings decently. When circumstances caused him to do less than this, he was deeply ashamed. But about who he was he refused to be ashamed.

Whatever the reason for his departure from Tulane, he left with dignity. He did not flee New Orleans in disgrace. For the rest of his life he liked to keep in touch with friends in that city. And his friends there did not desert him. Three of his good friends in New Orleans, all prominent women, had joined him in Taxco within two years. Spratling may have moved to Mexico for the same reasons others did—because it was beautiful and cheap and he liked the life, and after October 1929, there were few good jobs to be had at home. But the abrupt departure, the rumors, and the book review flung in the face of his critics as he left, suggest that Mexico was for him, as it has been for others whose unconventional sexual arrangements are frowned upon by North American puritans, a refuge.

CHAPTER TWO

THE ÉMIGRÉ FROM NEW ORLEANS

Taxco was at a low point in its history in 1929. The population was 3,254, down by a quarter from what it had been during the Borda years in the eighteenth century. The town had endured the decay of the mines, then the political upheavals of the nineteenth century, then the turmoil of the revolution. It was inhabited largely by old people, women, and children. Most of the men had gone to look for work elsewhere. Signs of poverty were everywhere. Houses built in the Borda era were gutted with age, decaying, overgrown with vegetation. Several had been turned into *mesons,* small inns that put up mule-drivers and their animals, and one had been converted to a small hotel, the Posada Doña Maria. Many people, too poor to pay the rents demanded for better quarters, lived in less, in windowless small shacks with dirt floors and thatched roofs. For rents were still demanded, mercilessly, by two pious women who had large land holdings.

Five or six Spanish families ran the small shops located around the town plaza—a boot shop called the Golden Boot, a hardware store, a grocery. On Sundays, market day, miners and Indians from hamlets off in the mountains gathered in the shade of the Indian laurels in the plaza to trade and buy supplies.

Living in Taxco was very cheap, which was a good thing, for Bill Spratling was, not for the first time in his life, living hand to mouth. He planned to support himself with his pen, by writing and sketching. He had a two-hundred-dollar advance from a publisher in New York for a book about life in a small Mexican town. He intended to supplement that with more articles for architectural journals and the monthly column on literary activity in Mexico for Irita Van Doren's book section in the Sunday *New York Herald Tribune.*

He moved into a house on the Calle Veracruz below the square which he rented from Victoria Vasquez. Then, within a few months, thanks to his friendship with the United States ambassador to Mexico, Dwight L. Morrow, he managed to buy a home of his own. Spratling had become friendly with Morrow, his wife Elizabeth, and their daughters during his summers in Mexico. As Morrow neared the end of his time in Mexico, he wanted to make a gift to the Mexican people. 19

20

William Spratling, "Taxco—city of the viceroys," published in *Architecture*, February 1929. © 1929 by the McGraw-Hill Companies, reproduced by permission of the publisher. Photo courtesy of Graduate School of Design, Harvard University.

Spratling suggested that he hire Diego Rivera to paint murals on Cortés's Palace in Cuernavaca, and he helped Diego work out a fee that included a two-thousand-dollar commission for himself. When Diego Rivera got the job, Spratling got the commission. It was the beginning of a pattern that would provide him with most of his livelihood in Mexico—to be the middle-man between those who wanted something, often after he had suggested to them that they might want it, and those who could provide it. He used this first large commission to buy himself a

house just up from the plaza in Taxco. It was to be his home for the next sixteen years.

The house was at 23 Calle de las Delicias (Street of Delights), and it became immediately his hearth, his delight, the center of his life. He bought the house from a local widow, Margarita Torrescano, who lived around the corner. It was small and very simple, but it had a large garden. The simplicity of the house was part of its charm—and part of what would become the Spratling mystique—that he always managed to live well, even elegantly, in very simple surroundings. The house and garden were surrounded by streets on three sides with a *barranca* (ravine) at the back. The garden had two different levels and many trees, including an Indian laurel from which, many years before, cuttings had been taken for the Indian laurels in the plaza. Spratling immediately began making improvements, working with the local craftsmen. He added an extra bedroom at the top and a lookout tower over the entrance. Later when he expanded the house to include a small apartment for Elizabeth Anderson he turned the *barranca* into a small swimming pool into which he could dive almost directly from his bed.

William Spratling, "The Plaza, Taxco," published in *Architecture*, February 1929. © 1929 by the McGraw-Hill Companies, reproduced by permission of the publisher. Photo courtesy of Graduate School of Design, Harvard University.

As a householder, Spratling became a recognized member of the community. He got to know the local bricklayers, the plumber, the electrician. He shopped in the local stores. He patronized the local bar, run by a woman named Berta. And slowly, the neighbors and the town made him one of them.

One neighbor, Efrim Domínguez, took him on horseback up into the mountains to the nearby Nahua Indian town of Tlamacazapa. There he was allowed to see, but not to photograph, a pre-Columbian codex. Spratling made a tracing of it which he sent back to Franz Blom in the archaeology department at Tulane, and he talked about it enough to get some local publicity. "Spratling discovers an important códice," a Mexican newspaper reported.[1]

The Morrows came to visit him at his house. Elizabeth Morrow wrote in her journal:

> Saturday, August 23, 1930. Today we went to Taxco. Bill Spratling took us and we went straight to his house, a tiny place perched on the hill. A blue gate covered with pink bigonia [sic] opens into a crowded patio, full of coffee plants and vines. The house has a sala, a bedroom, a corridor and two piazzas. We ate on the back one hung with grinning masks and screened by vines. A sweet little deer, a green parrot, and a duck keep Bill company. His man-of-all-work gave us hot soup, frijoles and chicken and there was music afterwards. A carpenter, painter and a leather man came and sat on the garden wall and played old Mexican songs on two guitars and a flute. All the neighborhood children danced below the wall in the street.[2]

Eventually Spratling hired a cook, Eugenia, and a gardener, Juanito, and they gave him additional entrees into small-town Mexico. One night he fell down the steep stairs in his house, dislocating his hip and his jaw and breaking three ribs. When Eugenia found him the next morning, she went to fetch a curandera (a native healer specializing in bone pulling). She brought back a small wizened old lady who, grinning and pulling, got Spratling's joints back in place and taped his ribs.[3]

Although Taxco was isolated and distant from the capital city, gradually a few visitors found their way there. Some were intellectuals from Mexico City who had recently discovered the town, drawn by its picturesqueness, the spring-like year-around climate, the dazzling beauty of the local parish church, and not least perhaps, by its difficulty of access. Visitors came on horseback or took the train to El Naranjo and a horse or automobile on from there until 1928 when the road between Mexico City and Acapulco was opened. Moisés Sáenz fell in love with

Spratling holding young deer, 1930. Carl Zigrosser Papers, Special Collections, Van Pelt Library, University of Pennsylvania.

Taxco and asked Spratling to design a house for him there. Another of the town's partisans and publicists was the colonial art historian Manuel Toussaint. He asked Spratling to do the illustrations for a book he was writing about Taxco.

The Mexican government also had discovered the town—as an isolated place to which political troublemakers might be allowed to go. David Alfaro Siqueiros arrived in Taxco on probation and on bail in November 1930, after having spent six months in a penitentiary in Mexico City. He had been arrested for taking part in a violent May Day demonstration, although Spratling reported, in one of his "Literary Notes from Mexico" columns in the book section of the *New York Herald Tribune,* that it was simply part of a Mexican government crackdown on "Communists" and that Siqueiros was not a member of the Communist Party nor even politically active at the time. Spratling helped Siqueiros publish a group of thirteen woodcuts he had done in prison and wrote a preface to the book. With others he encouraged Siqueiros to take up oil painting again, which Siqueiros had nearly abandoned, and they arranged for an exhibition in Mexico City in January

David Alfaro Siqueiros,
lithograph of Spratling, 1931.
Photo courtesy of Sucesores
de William Spratling, S.A.

1932, the first solo public exhibition Siqueiros had had. Siqueiros showed some specifically Taxco subjects, such as "Head of a Miner" and "Mining Accident," as well as a head and chest nude "Portrait of William Spratling," which the subject thought was "simply great."[4] Siqueiros's year in Taxco was one of the most artistically productive of his life, but it ended as abruptly as it had begun. During his exhibition in Mexico City, he made a speech condemning the debasing of folk art into tourist art, which he regarded as a form of imperialistic penetration. Because making speeches was a violation of the terms of his probation, he was asked to leave Mexico, and did so, accepting an invitation to teach in Los Angeles.[5] By that time Spratling was not sorry to see him go. He had loaned him an amount of money he could not afford with no hope of ever getting it back, and he had come to realize that Diego Rivera and David Siqueiros were so jealous of one another that friendship with both of them was virtually impossible.[6]

The friendship with Diego Rivera was important to him, for Diego introduced him to Mexico as Spratling in turn was introducing Diego to the United States. Spratling's first interest in Mexico had been colonial church architecture, but Diego Rivera taught him to look at primitive and folk art, especially the art of the Indians, as the true art of Mexico. Spratling's circle of friends in Mexico City included Diego Rivera and Miguel Covarrubias, along with the Morrows, an American expatriate from Chicago named Frederick Davis, and a penniless young Austrian count named René d'Harnoncourt. All of them were making collections of Mexican folk art—pottery, jewelry, carved wooden toys, tin work, weavings, the masks used in Indian dances. Under their influence Spratling shifted his attention to the folk arts of Mexico.

A hastily written column he sent back to the *New York Herald Tribune* in early June 1930, describes his activities. He called it "The Arts and Letters in Mexico":

> March and April are good months to be in Mexico, particularly for writers. During these months there are many important Indian fiestas—the kind of things that make one wonder how the capital of this country presumes to consider itself really Mexican in comparison with indigenous Mexico. These fiestas take place in remote villages . . . yet they are frequently attended by thirty to fifty thousand Indians. Susan Smith, René d'Harnoncourt and I recently went to a fiesta at Tepalcingo, in the southern part of the state of Morelos. . . . Little Spanish was spoken. One heard Aztec, Otomi, and Zapotec. There were artisans and merchants from at least six states. Lacquer from Olinala, earthenware from Oaxaca and the Valle de la Luz, gold trinkets from Iguala and Acapulco, rebozos from Chilapa, serapes, petates and a thousand other things were there. . . .
>
> Then there was the feria and fiesta of Tecalpulco, just below Taxco. Stuart Chase and Marion Tyler enjoyed that. And the week before Easter I went to Chalma, three days on horseback above here, to see the famous religious dances. . . . Diego Rivera was there.[7]

The state of Guerrero is known for its traditional dances. Spratling began to collect the masks used in these dances, and he lined the walls of his house with them. One of his best masks came from nearby Tehuilotepec, where a local man had found it buried in the dirt in a pig pen. Spratling bought it from him for a few pesos.[8] When he wanted something badly enough, he could be devious. Enrique Alferez, today a well-known sculptor in New Orleans, remembers meeting Spratling in Taxco in 1930 when Alferez was on his way to work with Franz Blom in the Yucatan. Spratling took him along to visit a local peasant family who had several valuable inherited masks which they refused to sell. "This is Dr. Alferez," he said to the woman whose husband was ill, implying that he had brought Alferez to treat him, and Alferez, caught off guard and embarrassed, muttered some standard advice about fresh air and proper food. The woman was so grateful that she called her son to get a ladder and bring the masks down from the beams of the house where they were stored. Spratling got them for nothing.[9]

He also collected pottery. For a time around 1930 he decided that clay was his favorite medium. He bought clay pots, many from small villages off in the mountains, and helped Dwight Morrow make a collection of them which was to go on exhibit at the Metropolitan Museum of Art in New York.

But clay did not hold his interest for long. Diego Rivera gave him his first piece of pre-Columbian sculpture, "a tiny stone face with a slant jaw which he called a 'pre-Hispanic Spratling.'"[10] As Spratling traveled through the mountains to distant villages on horseback, he was offered (and began to buy) more of these small archaeological pieces. They soon became his passion.

For the first year Spratling was in Taxco, he and a newspaperman named Jaime Plenum were the only Americans in town. But others soon came, many of them drawn by his enthusiasm. In Mexico City he had met the folklorist Frances (Paca) Toor, who came immediately to visit him after he had settled in Taxco. She was the editor of *Mexican Folkways,* a magazine with texts in Spanish and English that was designed to attract North American tourists to Mexico and was partially supported by the Mexican government. Spratling took her to a three-day festival at the local Veracruz church and to a private religious shrine owned by one Doña Dolores Sanchez, and he showed her the house he had designed for Moisés Sáenz. All of these were duly featured in her magazine, accompanied by Spratling's drawings.[11]

Novelist Susan Smith moved to Taxco for several months and wrote *The Glories of Venus* (the name of a cantina) which featured a Spratling-like character. Katherine Anne Porter considered moving to Taxco and stayed briefly in Spratling's house while he was away in Mexico City. John Evans, Mabel Dodge Luhan's son, and his wife bought a house in Taxco and loaned it for a time to Andrew Dasburg, a painter from New Mexico. Writer Carleton Beals visited Taxco several times. In his memoirs Beals remembered Spratling in a restaurant with friends, one of whom, Lee Simonson, the editor of *Creative Arts,* was digging at him. Spratling finally had had enough. He grabbed a piece of paper and made a swift caricature of Simonson, a caricature so brilliant and so brutal that the group sat stunned.[12]

Stuart Chase and his wife Marion Tyler stopped in Taxco going to and from Acapulco, and according to Spratling Chase conceived the idea for his best-selling book, *Mexico: A Study of Two Americas* (1931) during a sleepless night on a straw pallet on Spratling's living room floor.[13] In his book Chase compares the neurosis-inducing "machine-made" civilization of the United States with what he took to be the greater serenity of Indian Mexico, where every man had his own corn plot and unemployment was not a worry. Chase took much of the information in his book from anthropologist Robert Redfield's study of Tepoztlán, an Indian village near Cuernavaca, but his theme—and his sympathetic identification with Mexico—were sealed during his brief stay with Spratling.

Stuart Chase wrote, "I stood on the top of a mountain in Guerrero, while Mr. William Spratling pointed out to me a remote castellated ridge, on the crest of which he had located seven pyramids, unknown to archaeologists."[14]

Chase witnessed and described a dance that can still be seen, in the 1990s, on festival days in Taxco:

> . . . the famous tiger dance . . . performed in the courtyard of a hillside
> chapel by a group of Indians arrayed in masks and special costumes, to the
> music of drum and pipe played simultaneously by a single musician. For
> hours the pipe wove its primitive tune, the drum thumped its stirring,
> monotonous rhythm, and the dancers, surrounded by a dense ring of
> enchanted Indians, stamped out the long and involved story of the tiger
> [jaguar] hunt.[15]

Afterward everyone filed into the chapel for mass and then returned to the churchyard for a fiesta with food stalls, a band, acrobats, and fireworks. Chase marveled at its mix of "Aztec dance, Roman mass, itinerant circus, all enacted . . . in a fairly sophisticated town as Mexican towns go."[15]

Chase also commented on his host:

> the inquiring traveler . . . is bound to spend long evenings in the company
> of compatriots who have gone virtually native, listening as they remove
> cover after cover from the surface of Mexico until he stares dizzily into a
> bottomless pit of mysteries. . . . Beyond that mountain lies a village. . . .

28

Sometimes you can hear the drums. . . . You saw these herb charms in the market? . . . Being simpatico is not enough, you have to establish confianza[trust] . . .[16]

"The village beyond the mountain," "the drums," "the herbs in the market," "establishing confianza"—these are all Spratling themes. Chase appears to have recorded, almost verbatim, snatches of conversations in Spratling's living room.

A year later, when Spratling's own book had appeared and Chase was asked to review it, he remembered again the unsettling sense of mystery, of living on the edge of unplumbed depths, that he had felt in Spratling's house in Taxco:

On the Street of the Delights lives Mr. Spratling, and when I first saw him he had a live faun in his little patio, an Indian boy to fry frijoles above the braziers of his tiny kitchen, and a most gorgeous and horrendous array of dance masks upon his walls. Throughout the day and night muffled Indians would knock upon his door with news, whispered in soft Spanish, of treasure trove, preconquest jade, buried pyramids and far villages where pots are made with all the cunning of five hundred years ago. To stay in this house is to live on the brink of mystery, appealing, unfathomable and sometimes a little fearful.[17]

Natalie Scott arrived in Taxco in the summer of 1930. She came to ride horses (she was an expert horsewoman) and to live more cheaply than she could in New Orleans. She threw herself into Taxco life, acting as a local realtor, giving parties for the North American tourists, and organizing a day nursery for the local mothers. Caroline Durieux from New Orleans, whose husband was with General Motors in Mexico, came to Taxco to paint. Then Elizabeth Anderson appeared. She was divorced from Sherwood and rather at loose ends when she ran into Bill Spratling in Mexico City in 1931. He insisted that she visit Taxco with him. When she got there, he persuaded her to stay. Eventually he created an apartment for her in his own house. "I really loved Sherwood . . . but he got tired of me and there was nothing more to do about it. It was as simple as that," she told a young friend in 1947.[18] In Taxco she found a new life, and she stayed there until she died in 1976.

Spratling liked older women, particularly those as intelligent, cultured, and witty as Elizabeth Anderson was, and his combination of southern gallantry and sensitivity, even vulnerability, attracted them in turn. Several older women were among his best friends. In Mexico City there was Elizabeth Morrow, the wife of the ambassador, who asked him to make drawings of their weekend house in Cuernavaca for a small book whose text she would write. In New Orleans it had

William Spratling at home, c. 1932. Studio Juarez, Taxco. Photo courtesy of the family of Margarita Domínguez Islas.

The small photo on the wall to the right is of Spratling's father, Dr. William P. Spratling.

been the painter Caroline Durieux who took him around to art galleries, his landlady Natalie Scott who got him invited to the right parties and mentioned him frequently in her society column, and Elizabeth Anderson. Now the latter three were all in Taxco.

Spratling's relations with these women were fraternal. They were like honorary older sisters, to whom he transferred some of his feelings for his mother and his older sister Lucille. He wanted to share his discoveries with them. He liked to do favors for them. But the favors had to be his idea, not something they had suggested. His independence was his most precious possession.

Elizabeth Anderson was surprised at the change that Mexico had made in Bill Spratling. He was more expansive, more lively and self-assertive than he had been in New Orleans, where his role was the quiet sidekick while Sherwood Anderson or William Faulkner held forth. When I mentioned this "expansiveness" to anthropologist Gobi Stromberg, she nodded. "I've seen it so many times in Americans who have just come to Mexico," she said. She attributed it to the Mexicans' love of solving practical problems, a "can-do" attitude, which makes an outsider suddenly feel that all things are possible.[19]

In the summer of 1931 a twenty-four-year-old art student and puppeteer from Minneapolis, Donald Cordry, turned up in Taxco. Cordry was "a tall young man of singular physical beauty" and a romantic who liked to say that he lived "only for beauty."[20] He and Spratling became very good friends, lovers, according to local gossip. They explored Guerrero on horseback, visiting remote mountain villages where the people spoke only Nahua or one of the other Indian languages, and hamlets deep in the tropical river valleys. Spratling bought more archaeological pieces, "idols" the people called them, which he could get for a few pesos each from the campesinos. He also added to his collection of masks. Cordry especially liked the masks, which were closely related to his puppets. He eventually wrote the book *Mexican Masks* and then with his wife, Dorothy Mann, whom he married in 1936, a book entitled *Mexican Indian Costumes.*

In the fall of 1931 Spratling purchased two horses at Ometepec, on the lower coast of Guerrero for 75 pesos each, he wrote to his friend William Zigrosser in New York.[21] He wanted Zigrosser, who was working for an art gallery, to sell some watercolors by Diego Rivera for him if possible, because he needed the money. In Taxco Spratling hired a tall and very handsome young Mexican, Jenaro Díaz, to take care of the horses. Then he bought two more and broke them in with Díaz. The horses became an excuse for more extended trips in the mountains. Spratling and Jenaro Díaz made long explorations together all over the state of Guerrero, with Díaz acting as Spratling's adjutant, guide, and bodyguard. "Mr. Spratling was very, very fond of Jenaro," Antonio Castillo told me.[22] Others in Taxco were blunter. "Jenaro Díaz was the great love of Spratling's life," an older man sitting in a bar said.

It was an idyllic life, with Spratling entertaining guests from Mexico and the United States, working on his book, making long trips on horseback, and adding always to his collection of Mexican crafts and archaeological pieces. Mexican folk art, he thought, would be the subject of his next book.

John Dos Passos, whom Spratling had known in New Orleans, came to visit and insisted on going horseback riding. Afterwards, to recuperate, they went to Berta's to try tequila mixed with lemonade. It became a "Berta," a standard drink in Taxco and later all over Mexico.[23]

Hart Crane spent several weekends at Spratling's house in Taxco in 1931. He succumbed to the craze for Mexican folk art like everyone else and bought serapes, giant hats, embroideries, lacquer trays, and pottery. "You've never seen such beautiful arts and crafts as the Indian element here has perpetuated," he wrote a friend. "Wm. Spratling's collection at Taxco is one of the best."[24] To another friend Crane joked about Spratling's "precious collection of timeless, or rather dateless, idols."[25]

Spratling's only immediate problem was money. The advance for the book had long been spent. His columns for Irita Van Doren dwindled away. To Zigrosser in June of 1930 he confessed to being ghastly broke.[26] For a time he lived hand to mouth, much like the poorer local people did, without a bank account. When he needed a check, he bought one from Natalie Scott. When he needed a loan, he got one from Berta at the local bar. But he was resourceful, as he had learned to be years before when he became an orphan. He found prominent patrons, including Moisés Sáenz and Dwight and Elizabeth Morrow, all of whom paid him for various small jobs. He earned some much-needed cash by renting out his four horses at two pesos a day to what he contemptuously called the tourist rabble.[27] And he began to sell whatever he could get his hands on. He offered art works to a gallery in New York—watercolors by Diego Rivera, works by Siqueiros, his own drawings, and already, at this early date, some archaeological pieces. By the fall of 1931 when he finished his book, he was living on rent from the horses, plus a small amount advanced to him for the archaeological pieces by the New York gallery. All he needed to do, he thought, was to get by until his book made him some money.

By 1931 there was a small community of expatriates in Taxco. Hart Crane described to a friend:

> . . . a small group of quite interesting compatriots here which gathers
> occasionally at one or the other of our houses . . . Carleton Beals and wife;
> Anita Brenner; Marsden Hartley, the painter, who has just arrived and
> who is wildly enthusiastic; Lesley Simpson (University of California) and

wife; Wm. Spratling, whose book Little Mexico (just out) you ought to read, etc.[28]

Elsewhere Crane wrote, "Taxco is so extremely beautiful—and the townsfolk still so affable—that whatever one has to say about the yankee occupation (and that ultimately seals its doom) its still one of the pleasantest places to be."[29]

Witter Bynner was more critical. In 1931 he found Taxco "beautiful beyond description, with cobblestones lanes leading always up and up into a hundred little heavens, all at strange angles, and the huge ornate church standing in the center like the giant parent of eight other small churches" but the American households in Taxco he thought were "all semi-crazy and completely drunken."[30]

Aldous Huxley had the same complaint: "Taxco is largely inhabited by artists and by those camp-followers of the arts whose main contribution to the cause of Intellectual Beauty consists in being partially or completely drunk for several hours each day."[31]

But Elizabeth Anderson remembered it differently: in Mexico everyone seemed to be working. Bill Spratling was writing *Little Mexico* and creating jewelry designs; Caroline Durieux was working at paintings that would later be shown at the Museum of Modern Art in New York; Donald Cordry was collecting and studying the native crafts in Guerrero, and Tamara Schee had a ballet school. Even Natalie Scott was writing a book about her life.

She never did finish it, but she worked on it furiously, writing in a scrawled hand that was illegible, even to her. She made notes constantly and shuffled them around until they were hopelessly scrambled, and she would have to spend an entire day trying to find out where, exactly, she was in the story of her life. By the time she had gotten her notes in order, she was too exhausted to do anything but throw a party.[32]

LITTLE MEXICO

Little Mexico by William Spratling, with a foreword by Diego Rivera, was published by Harrison Smith in New York and Jonathan Cape in London early in 1932. The author had hoped to go to New York for the publication, but he could not afford the trip. So he waited impatiently in Taxco, eager to hear what his friends in New York, including Diego Rivera, who was there at the time, were saying about it. He begged William Zigrosser to write him critically about the book and to let him know what Diego thought.[1]

Diego Rivera had already written a letter which Spratling had used as a foreword to the book. In it he had praised the "acuteness and grace" of Spratling's "many small portraits of people and things" and compared them to portraits "painted by certain masters in my country who died before I was born. Those portraits were made with precision and tenderness and contain irony and love." It sounded like generous praise, and perhaps it was, but Diego was not completely to be trusted, Spratling knew. He was erratic, jealous of any one else's fame, and notorious for holding contradictory opinions simultaneously. Spratling obviously worried about what Diego was really saying about the book to their mutual friends in New York.

What Spratling had at stake was not just his financial well-being but his reputation as a writer. Desperate for money, he hoped that the book would be a financial success. But more important to him was that the book be respected by the people he respected. His good friends were among the foremost writers and artists in the United States and Mexico: William Faulkner, Sherwood Anderson, John Dos Passos, Diego Rivera, Miguel Covarrubias. Spratling was a proud man. He wanted to be an equal in this company. But was he? Had he succeeded in the difficult task he had set himself, which was to write a book about small town Mexican life from the inside, as it was experienced by the local people? Or had he, a gringo, been presumptuous in attempting to write about the real Mexico? Only a Mexican could set his mind at rest on that question, which is why he was so eager to know what Diego Rivera was saying.

PANCHO Y SU HERMANO.   PANCHO AND HIS BROTHER.

Little Mexico begins in a bar in Taxco where two North American salesmen are exchanging bits of misinformation about Mexico's history. Having set the stage— how little gringo*s* know about the real Mexico—Spratling described the place as he experienced it—the town, the hot country below, the cold mountains above, the local fiestas. There follow portraits of eight of the local people in Taxco. One is Juanito, Spratling's young gardener, who liked to talk and would sit absorbed for hours recounting to Spratling the events of his life. Another is an old revolutionary turned tax collector, Jesús Llorado, who wrote florid poetry and liked to give public orations. There is pious Doña Petra, the local capitalist, who rented out many small parcels of land to poor peasants and loaned money at 20 percent interest per month, and Doña Maria, the prosperous owner of a private religious shrine much visited by Indians who brought offerings and hoped for miracles. There is the highly respected local artist, Maestro Ayala, a painter of miracle paintings and carver of masks, who told Spratling his troubles with women, and

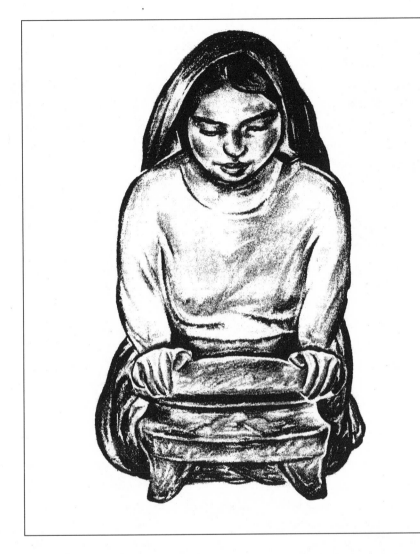

William Spratling, "Lola," from *Little Mexico*, 1932, republished as *A Small Mexican World* (Boston: Little Brown, 1964). Reproduced by permission of Little, Brown and Company.

Tata (Daddy) Luis, ninety years old, the bell-ringer at Santa Prisca who knew the priest's secrets. There is Lola, twenty years old, with four children by as many fathers, who cooked for Spratling for three pesos a week, although at first she worried about what people would say if she went to work for a single man. And finally there is Galindo, the idealistic young Indian teacher at the local school, an agrarian reformer and a proponent of rural education. Spratling sometimes sketched the students in his class, and on Saturdays they would go swimming in the pool at the bottom of a *barranca* below the town. The word-portraits are sympathetic, but slightly distanced, almost objective in tone. Not surprisingly, they show the influence of William Faulkner.

The sixteen sketches Faulkner wrote for the *Times-Picayune* while he was in New Orleans were slight, but in them Faulkner seemed to be "trying to write a kind of anthropological study of New Orleans people and places," one of his biographers noted. Faulkner had read some of Frazier's *The Golden Bough,* and he tried to do something similar, "to distance himself from his material and perceive his subject matter as a researcher might view another culture."[2] His subjects reflected life in the French Quarter at the time: bootleggers, race-track touts, a jockey, a crippled beggar, a restaurant owner, a young hoodlum, and he treated them with respect and sympathy, recognizing, as one critic has noted, "their hunger—for recognition, for love, and for dignity."[3]

After Faulkner left New Orleans, Spratling had tried the same kinds of sketches or word-portraits to accompany his drawings. He had tested the technique in two articles for *Scribner's Magazine,* his "Cane River Portraits" and "Figures in a Mexican Renaissance."

In *Little Mexico* he again did these honest, sympathetic, but objective portraits, occasionally touched with irony. His subject was the same as Faulkner's: commonplace but unique characters in a particular, local setting.

A second influence on Spratling was contemporary anthropology. He was experimenting with a new genre. First-hand field-work reports on daily life in a "primitive" society had recently produced some unexpected best-sellers in the United States. The best known was Margaret Mead's *Coming of Age in Samoa,* which had appeared in 1926. But there were others, including *Life in Lesu* by Hortense Powdermaker, *Sex and Repression in Savage Society* by Bronislaw Malinowski, and Robert Redfield's *Tepoztlán: A Mexican Village,* which Stuart Chase had used in writing his more popular *Mexico: A Study of Two Americas.* Between 1929 and 1931, when Spratling was sending columns to Irita Van Doren for the *New York Herald Tribune,* Margaret Mead's colleague Ruth Benedict reviewed a book on anthropology or archaeology there nearly every week. To read Benedict's reviews, which Spratling likely did, would have been the equivalent of a short course in contemporary anthropology, with the emphasis on cultural relativism, on appreciating non-Western cultures, and on the potential *usefulness* of anthropology in suggesting how Westerners might improve their own society.

Spratling behaved very much like an anthropologist. He went to a foreign place, settled in to live among the people, and tried to experience their world, to learn what they thought about things, and then to convey this as succinctly and accurately as possible. Interwoven among the eight portraits are short essays on various topics (the town, fiestas, the harvest cycle, local legends) that round out his picture of local life. He captures the feeling of a small town—the gossip, the folk beliefs, the commonly held opinions. In a later edition published in 1964 he changed the title from *Little Mexico* to *A Small Mexican World,* the better to convey what the book was really about, which was the "culture," as anthropologists would have said, of small-town Mexico.

But Spratling wanted *Little Mexico* to be more than portraits, more than ethnographic description. He wanted it to have adventure, journeys, a personal narrative, and so he began with his own experience of the town on a typical late afternoon and evening and with accounts of his journeys down the Balsas River into the *tierra caliente* (the hot country), by horseback up into the *tierra fría* (the cold country, the mountains), and of visits to fiestas. These journeys, particularly his trip into the *tierra caliente,* are the emotional heart of the book. He abandoned his objective pose to write not of what he observed but of what he felt, and what he felt stirred him deeply.

Taxco lies just inside the northern border of the state of Guerrero, a wild land of windswept peaks, steamy tropical river valleys, and hot, dry coastland, of impoverished and resentful peoples, traditionally a land of bandits and revolutionaries. South of the Sierra de Taxco mountain range in which Taxco lies is a deep chasm cut by the Rio Balsas and the Rio Mezcala, a low-lying river valley extending east and west across the state of Guerrero which has the hottest year-round climate in all of Mexico. Beyond that is the Sierra Madre del Sur, a forbidding range of mountains, "seemingly marching southward like the waves of the sea," as Spratling later wrote.[4] This is the countryside in which his book is set.

Spratling reveled in the *tierra caliente,* this "Mexico unknown even to the Mexicans." He called it "the country's physical subconscious." It was "vast and fecund; forbidding and promising . . . practically unexplored and difficult of access."[5] The geography of the place, isolated and exhausting to move through, excited him, as did the mixture of people he encountered and the archaeological treasures he stumbled upon. There is a tropical sensuousness in his writing—a glorying in the body's sensations of thirst, sweat, fatigue, hunger satisfied by beans and tortillas, and male camaraderie around a fireside. He went down the Balsas with a companion who is unnamed, but the pleasure, even exaltation he so obviously felt suggest that the person accompanying him may have been Jenaro Díaz.

Their journey began where the Balsas River crosses the federal road directly south of Iguala. They left in the dark at four in the morning, climbing silently into the wooden boat already holding two sets of oarsmen, ten passengers, mostly Mexicans, and a cargo of little pigs. Their "Noah's Ark," as Spratling called it, their "wooden box of a boat, shaped a little like a coffin" moved swiftly through deep gorges, over rapids, and around boulders. In the dim light of early morning he studied the oarsmen. They were "slender but with broad shoulders" with "features rather fine, as in Aztec masks." They were barefoot in soiled white pants rolled up to the knees and white shirts "open down the front revealing lavender or pink undershirts against bronze skin." Even if he had nothing to keep in it each man wore a *huichol* or money sack "over secret parts, falling as a small black triangle between straining thighs." Laughing, they called it a "sheep."

En route they met the crew of another boat, laboriously hauling their craft upstream. For every day of downward journey, Spratling learned, there was eight to fifteen days of back-breaking pull upstream. The oarsmen had to begin very young, he was told, in order to get used to the hardship of it.

They passed small villages: Tetela-del-Rio, where they bought mezcal, Santo Tomás, Santa Rosa, Xochitepec, El Cubo. Beyond the river to the south and west were the mountain ranges of the Sierra Madre, shades of metallic blue in the distance. On the map that whole region was marked "unexplored." Late in the afternoon they reached San Miguel Totolapan, the commercial center of the *tierra caliente,* where a fiesta was in progress and they were served frijoles, tortillas, broiled chicken, good beer from Orizaba, and locally grown coffee. They were the only outsiders in the town. Everyone else appeared to be pure Indian—Aztec and Tarascan. But they could not linger, for it was six hours more on the river to Ajutchitlán where they would spend the night.

Ajutchitlán had been a large town before the revolution passed through, leaving its big houses vacant and abandoned, the patios overgrown with weeds. The people who remained lived in stick and mud huts, tended small plots of corn and beans, and during the dry season made pottery from the mud of the riverbank. Spratling was very taken with the pottery—casseroles and water jars and incense burners with a fine hard deep green glaze and some "common ware" from the next village, Changato, decorated with drawings that reminded him of the pre-Colonial codices he had seen in the National Museum in Mexico City. He bought as much as he could carry.

At Ajutchitlán they hired mules and a young boy to drive them and crossed barren hills in search of an ancient temple and an old man who had idols for sale. The expedition was frustrating. The old man named fantastic prices for his few crude pieces and finally refused to sell. The temple was a large vague mass. "Here is work for archaeologists," Spratling acknowledged. "We leave it to press onward."

Back at Ajutchitlán they took another boat on down the river and through rapids to Pungarabato. With mules they set out again in search of ruins. One route led through mountain passes where travelers were regularly held up by bandits. Their guide rode with a carbine across his saddle. Spratling carried a pistol. Another day they found ruined temples and pyramids at Cútzeo and Cuirícuaro near Huetamo. They bought lacquered gourds and at Almoloya a stone mask encrusted with turquoise "like the one in the National Museum" from an innkeeper who let them have it for five pesos. Above Acapetlahuaya there were more ruins, the foundations of a city cut out of solid rock. From a high point they looked out at the surrounding mountains and down below at the serpentine coils of the Rio Balsas. Then overland by burro and horseback they made the long journey back to Taxco.

Tierra fría, the mountain fastness around Taxco, also yielded adventures—and treasures, although Spratling's tone is colder in describing these mountain journeys than when he was glorying in the sensuousness of the *tierra caliente.* He retells the story of the discovery of the codex that had already been announced in a Mexico City newspaper—how he and his neighbor went on horseback to a nearby Indian village which was rumored to have an old map, a pre-Columbian pictograph, painted on cloth. The map was produced, and Spratling was allowed to copy it. What the newspaper had not reported was the full context of the map-copying session. While Spratling was making the colored tracing of the map, three soldiers appeared. They started to arrest a fourth soldier, a young man who had been drinking in the cantina, and when the latter resisted, shot him in the back. The soldier fell and rolled over in the dirt, while the old men of the village stood silent, embarrassed. The owner of the map shrugged. "The army, señor . . . ," he explained.

On another expedition into the mountains Spratling lowered himself by rope down a hundred feet into a limestone cave where he found an Aztec pot, a few jadeite beads, and two small bronze hatchets. Another day he and two guides, whom he calls young Ysaías and old Don Carmen, went on horseback fifteen kilometers northwest of Taxco to a high mesa near Tetipac where they camped for a several days near ruined pyramid structures of cut stone. Along with scorpions and a *coralillo* (red poisonous snake), they found pottery shards, arrow heads, obsidian knives, and "two beautifully carved gods." One, a male figure, had an ear of corn in his left hand and an insignia in his right.

In a section on the town in *Little Mexico* Spratling describes nighttime serenades and a marijuana smoking session. In "Music in the Night" the theme is longing:

> The strains continue unrelentingly, making a thousand new beginnings,
> far into the night. The sound of the guitars is like wind in the trees and
> the flute and bass viol strain and pull with coaxing insistence. I finally go
> into the house.

For the marijuana session, Spratling and five friends, whom he calls the Chicken, Clay Man, the Siren, the Bun, and the Duck, hoisted themselves up onto the roof of the former Convent of San Bernardino. It is a stream-of-consciousness account, also influenced by Faulkner. Spratling and the others giggle and chatter. The world appears two-dimensional, and he feels as if he could reach out and touch the dome of Santa Prisca hanging in the air before him. Everything is funny, until the Bun falls off the roof, to land, fortunately, on the parapet and not down on the plaza below. Thirsty, they get water and drink it and with it return to the world of three dimensions.

42   *Little Mexico,* one man's personal odyssey into the soul of Mexico and into his own soul as well, is a small masterpiece. The author had worked on it for three and a half years. There are "two approaches to writing a book about a foreign country," he told an interviewer years later. "You can write it in all innocence after the first five days, the outsider approach. But if you want to stay longer, you have to put your roots in, do it from the inside out."[6] He had put down roots in Taxco and written his portraits of the local people "from the inside out."

Spratling illustrated the book with eighty-four drawings, sketches of the town, the market, the people who were the subjects of his word portraits, even the decorations on the pottery. In these he tried to capture the directness, the crudeness, the love, the honesty of folk art. His simple black-and-white drawings are so unique and so expressive of the text that *Little Mexico* was selected by the American Institute of Graphic Arts as one of the best illustrated American books for 1931–33.

Little Mexico is a small book—fewer than 200 pages, although he had written much more. When he was finished, he sat down with the manuscript and shortened it by nearly half, cutting out 132 pages. He was a man of few words, taciturn, sometimes chided by his friends for saying only about a word and a half about each thing, as Natalie Scott had once complained.[7] He wanted his book to be as succinct, blunt, plain speaking, as he was.

Little Mexico reflects its author in many other ways. It is not an idealized view of Mexico, but through it flows a romantic sensibility which finds the joys of life in nonmaterial things. Spratling lived most of his life in a very simple fashion. His house was small, his furniture only a few wooden chairs. He was able to capture, because he shared them, the values of a society little interested in consumption. "Mexican values are essentially spiritual and mystical," Gutierre Tibón, a longtime resident of Cuernavaca and the author of many books about Mexico, told me. "In *Little Mexico* William Spratling penetrated deeply into Mexico which otherwise is a mystery [and] opened new doors for Anglo-Saxon people."

Little Mexico reflects also Spratling's growing inclination, influenced by his friends in Mexico City, to play down the Spanish colonial legacy in Mexico in favor of the Indian legacy. Diego Rivera, Covarrubias, and Moisés Sáenz were all strongly anticolonial, and by the time Spratling moved to Taxco he had adopted their point of view. Of the baroque church of Santa Prisca, Spratling wrote, "It is a product of the inefficiently integrated colonization of short-sighted Spanish colonials and it long since ceased to be expressive of life here," an odd statement and scarcely true, for it is contradicted by many of the details in his portraits and by his general observation that the church takes up nearly all the time of the local women not devoted to housework. But Spratling had become more fascinated by Indian than by colonial Mexico. He wanted to stress what was indigenous in Taxco rather than what was Spanish and Roman Catholic.

There are no hints in *Little Mexico* that Spratling would soon be designing silver. Of the young idealist teacher, Spratling commented casually, as if this were of no more interest than any other of the many crafts being practiced in Taxco:

> Before he became a maestro [teacher] he was a silversmith in Iguala. He still treasures the tools of his trade and every now and then he can be found at work in the shade of his small patio fashioning a tiny pair of gold earrings for his baby girl or making his wife a collar of silver beads the size of marbles.

On the other hand, Spratling's interest in collecting archaeological pieces is much evident in *Little Mexico*. It is a thread that runs through the book, already one of the passions of his life.

Also present is a subtle homoeroticism, in the text and in the drawings. Several of the drawings celebrate male bodies and male faces. The women tend to be archetypes, more formal, impersonal. A young woman bent over the metate (corn-grinding stone) looks as if she herself is carved in stone. But the men are unique, warm, communicative.

None of the reviewers remarked directly on this aspect of the book, although Spratling's description of one woman did cause some comment. C. G. Poore, reviewing *Little Mexico* for the *New York Times* thought that Spratling was too hard on his own countrymen and women, especially the "lady writer" who does not understand how Mexican women can be content with their lives.[8] This provoked a reply from Spratling, who sent a letter to the *New York Times* to explain himself. About the North American woman writer, whom he had used as a foil for his cook, Lola, he insisted that he was only trying to contrast two distinct "feminine psychologies," not to suggest that one is wrong and the other right, but that here are two totally different ways of viewing the world.[9]

Yet the reviewer had noticed that the only sarcastic portraits in the book were of North American tourists. The artist Angel Ayala called the tourists *sincronizados*, Spratling reported slyly, because they were always looking at their watches. Spratling did not care much for the tourists either, and he particularly disliked the women. Spratling liked intelligent and independent women, but his contempt for most female tourists from the United States, especially if they had intellectual pretensions or asked silly questions, was a constant through his years in Mexico.

Caroline Durieux, painting of William Spratling, 1934. The Birmingham Museum of Art, Birmingham, Alabama; gift of Sarah d'Harnoncourt. The location of the original painting is not known.

He simply hated them. Caroline Durieux captured his attitude, including the cynicism with which he sold them silver in a portrait she painted of him in his shop in 1934. "They twitter," he would say, in disgust and as if in explanation.[10]

Stuart Chase's review in the *New York Herald Tribune* was more appreciative. "Mexico has claimed him," Chase wrote, and because of this "he can communicate its way of life with an understanding and a sympathy which no other North American to my knowledge possesses."[11]

In a second review in the *New York Times* in 1934, two years after the book was published, John Chamberlain ranked *Little Mexico* with the classic books on Mexico by Fanny Calderon de la Barca and Charles Flandreau and called it a work of "quirky charm." Mr. Spratling "has idled in the plaza, talked with Mexicans of all sorts, and reported the conversations back" for his readers. But Chamberlain too noted, "The only sort of person he doesn't like is the tourist . . . and the irony of Mr. Spratling's own life is that he is now making his living off tourists" by selling silver and serapes. Chamberlain thought it an irony appropriate for Mexico, a country that clung to the rhetoric of revolution while becoming rapidly more conservative.[12]

Little Mexico did not make Spratling's literary reputation. Nor did it end his financial troubles. He blamed his publishers, who were dissolving their partnership when his book appeared and made little attempt to sell it. But the book is not the sort that would have had large sales. It is a small gem, a work of ethnography such as a poet might write, a book of such subtle penetration that each reader likes to imagine that she or he alone has discovered it and holds it as a private treasure. It carries no message, unlike Stuart Chase's *Mexico: A Study of Two Americas,* which was a free-wheeling indictment of Western capitalist civilization and a paean to Mexican primitivism. Chase's book was unabashedly romantic. "Flowers are more important to Mexicans than are motor cars, radios, and bathtubs combined, to Americans," he wrote. "Middletown [USA] has its due quota of neurotic and mentally unbalanced individuals. In Tepoztlán a Freudian complex is unthinkable."[13] Chase's book appeared in 1931 just as Americans were wondering what had gone wrong in their lives, and it became a best-seller. Nor did Spratling make a memorable argument, as had Anita Brenner in the well-known *Idols Behind Altars* (1929), where she looked for spiritual continuity between ancient Mexicans, the revolutionary program, and the mural painters. Spratling's *Little Mexico* was a classic of honest understatement about the *mexicanitos,* the little people of Mexico. It appeared in 1932 and then disappeared almost immediately.

But it did not disappear completely. One by one, copies of the book found their way into the hands of sympathetic, even rapt, readers. In 1935 the poet Haniel Long in Santa Fe, New Mexico, wrote Spratling, who was a stranger to him, a five-page letter telling him how much *Little Mexico* meant to him and calling its author, perceptively, a new Walt Whitman.[14] Spratling kept that letter among his important papers for the rest of his life.

CHAPTER FOUR

Designs in Silver

Spratling waited in Taxco, flat broke, for the imagined royalties from his book. They never came. He complained to one friend that his electricity had been cut off and he could not even buy milk for his coffee.[1] Finally he decided to try his hand at what his friend and fellow expatriate Fred Davis was doing in Mexico City.

Frederick Davis had dropped out of medical school in Chicago and moved to Mexico City in 1910. He took a job with the Sonora News Company which ran the newsstands in Mexican train stations, and traveling around the country by train, he had become interested in Mexican arts and crafts. By 1926 when Spratling met him, Davis was a well-known collector of Mexican crafts and a dealer in antiques and contemporary painting. He also sold elegant silver jewelry which he had designed himself and contracted out for production. He sold the jewelry first in the Sonora News Company store in the grand Iturbide Hotel on Madero Avenue in Mexico City and later in a store of his own called Aztec Land across the street. His shop became an informal headquarters for artists and other expatriates in Mexico. Fred Davis also had a passion for remodeling houses and did at least ten in Mexico City, Cuernavaca, and Taxco, including one in Cuernavaca which he sold to Ambassador and Mrs. Morrow.[2]

Spratling knew Fred Davis well. They shared a friendship with the Morrows, as well as an interest in folk art and in remodeling houses. If he could produce a line of jewelry, he thought, Davis would sell it for him in Mexico City.

With this in mind, Spratling designed a silver ring with a stone set in it and took it to Iguala, forty kilometers from Taxco, which was a center for gold-working. Many of the goldsmiths there had been trained by Wenceslao Herrera, "the patriarch of the craftsmen," Spratling called him, "an old Indian who has the reputation of being the best silversmith in the state of Guerrero."[3] Spratling could see that technically the Iguala gold work was excellent, but he did not like the designs, mostly imitations of Spanish, Italian, and Portuguese work, with a lot of gold filigree.

Spratling gave his drawings to a young goldsmith, Artemio Navarrete, wanting   47

to see if he could handle contemporary designs. He liked what Navarrete produced, and prodded by Moisés Sáenz, David Alfaro Siqueiros, and Diego Rivera,
he wired Navarrete money for a round-trip ticket to Taxco, inviting him to come
and work for him.

When Navarrete appeared at his door, Siqueiros explained to him, "Bill has a
notion of opening a workshop right here in his home and you are the artisan who
can help him do it. We want you to live in Taxco so you can teach him your craft."[4]
Spratling offered Navarrete five times what he was earning in Iguala, and a week
later Navarrete moved to Taxco. He worked at a small table in Spratling's house,
melting one-peso coins in a brazier and turning out rings, half-moon earrings, and
belt buckles of Spratling's design. On weekends Spratling's friends, visiting from
Mexico City, bought up everything Navarrete had made. An all-weather road
linking Taxco with Cuernavaca had been completed in 1931, and that brought
more tourists. "When Americans came to visit Taxco, everybody would say, 'Let's
go see the gringo,' Antonio Castillo told me. He was the interpreter for the whole
town."[5] The people who came to have him interpret for them usually could be
persuaded to make purchases. Spratling found that he did not need to sell through
Fred Davis in Mexico City. He could create a market in Taxco for well-designed
hand-crafted silver.

Spratling shopped nearly every day at a hardware store, the Tlapalería Esmer-
aldo, just below his house on the town square, and the young son and nephews of
the proprietor liked to visit Spratling at his house, occasionally running errands
for him or Navarrete. One day the proprietress asked Spratling if he would tutor
her son, Salvador Terán, and her nephews Antonio, Jorge, and Justo Castillo, in
English. He agreed, and they began to come regularly for one hour a week. Before
and after the lesson they watched Navarrete at work. Navarrete showed them how
to wash and polish the silver and how to beat it into sheets. Eventually Spratling
hired them as apprentices, for thirty centavos a day, which they considered good
pay. The boys were between the ages of ten and sixteen. "We really wanted to learn
English, but we were interested in the silver," Antonio Castillo remembers.

The workshop grew phenomenally fast. Within months Spratling had rented
an old building down the street from his house, "a three-story semi-ruin with no
windows or doors or stairways, though the floors were intact."[6] It had been the old
customs house on the Camino Real, the royal road from Acapulco to Mexico City
which threaded its way through the town of Taxco. Spratling set up his workshop
on the upper two floors and kept his horses on the ground floor. He opened his
stop, the Taller de las Delicias, there on June 27, 1932. In addition to the silversmiths, Spratling had tinsmiths who produced lamps and mirrors and carpenters
who made simple heavy wood and leather furniture according to his designs. And

he had three families of weavers. One rainy night some weavers from Coatepec who were selling door to door in Taxco stopped at his house. He invited them in, offered them beer, and casually suggested they might someday come and set up 49 their looms in his workshop. Shortly thereafter they appeared, three families, with their looms and household goods loaded onto six mules. He moved them all into the former customs house.

The methods of silver-making in the early days were very simple. During the first year silver coins were melted down to make the jewelry. Later Spratling bought silver from miners who processed it in ovens on the hillsides near the mines and sold it from door to door in small bars wrapped in dirty cotton cloth. The metal was forged into sheets by hand and calibrated between the fingers, and soldering was done over a small wick flame from burning sesame seed oil.[7] Silver was cheap, but Spratling had to borrow the fifteen pesos from Bar Berta to buy his first kilo. When he needed money to meet his payroll, Berta would make him a loan. From these simple beginnings, his world-famous silver firm, which would bring fame and prosperity to Taxco, was born.

Within two years he had expanded across the street to the historic Verdugo house, where he had the display and salesroom on the upper level and his office below. By then he had forty employees. Navarrete had brought his brother-in-law, Alfonso Ruiz Mondragón, from Iguala as a second teacher, and Mondragón in turn brought his brother as a teaching assistant. A photograph celebrating the silver workshop on September 22, 1934 (Spratling's thirty-fourth birthday), shows two teachers, two teaching assistants, and fourteen young apprentices.

Spratling's first designs made use of ranch motifs such as ropes, straps, and balls, reflecting his interest in horses. Then he turned for inspiration to Mexican folk art and archaeology. He liked the simple, elegant shapes of good contemporary design, and he found that pre-Columbian and Mexican folk art were abstract enough to combine well with these. He had a large collection of clay seals that had been dug up in a brickyard outside Mexico City, and he used the abstract designs from these seals for brooches. He took a stylized turkey design from a painted clay pot and made of it a silver necklace. He used Mixtec designs from an ancient codex on money-clips and made brooches from the designs on the gold pieces that Alfonso Caso had just found in a tomb at Monte Albán.[8] He used the human hand as a motif, sometimes holding a flower, an image described by Anita Brenner in her book *Idols Behind Altars* as an ancient Mexican symbol. He made at least one item related to the intricate luxury pieces made by Aztec craftsmen which had so astonished Cortés and his men in the sixteenth century. The Spanish chroniclers described a silver monkey with moveable hands and feet which appeared to dance, a bird cast in silver that had a moveable head, tongue, and wings, and a fish

Silver workshop, 1934.
Private collection.

with alternating scales of gold and silver.[9] Spratling's version was a beautiful flexible silver fish pillbox with moveable scales.

Spratling liked to work in three dimensions, to consider his pieces as works of sculpture, and he had an architect's feeling for materials and their possibilities. Silver, he believed, should have "surface and body, plus a good convincing weight," unlike gold which is better worked delicately.[10] He liked a dull finish, which better showed the shape, but he soon learned that his women customers wanted jewelry that sparkled. "Subconsciously, a woman wears jewelry to attract the eye of the male," he said.[11] Earrings with a shiny finish always sold faster than those with a dull surface.

Spratling experimented with combinations of silver with other materials native to the region, such as rosewood and ebony, and with semiprecious stones, such as

William Spratling, silver bracelet, 1930s. Courtesy of Phyllis Goddard.

obsidian, malachite, amethyst quartz, and other quartzes, all of which were abundant in the mines around Taxco. For some inexplicable reason, he would say, silver is more beautiful when it is combined with these other products of the same soil than when it is used with diamonds or rubies, which make it appear "cold and insensitive."[12] He particularly liked the combination of amethyst with silver, but he preferred a local inexpensive orchid-colored amethyst with flaws to a pure (and expensive) deep purple Ural amethyst. It was partly an aesthetic decision and partly his sense of what was appropriate. Ebony was cheap and hard and black, but no one used it in Taxco. Spratling tried it, liked its look with silver, and hired a worker in ebony from Zacualpan, Fernando Carranza, who stayed with him for several years.[13]

Spratling's first designs were heavy, chunky, even crude. "I want it *feo* (ugly) like this," he would tell his workers. "Don't make it more beautiful."[14] Later his designs became lighter and more refined, as he used fewer pre-Columbian motifs and concentrated on developing whatever possibilities he saw in his materials,

William Spratling, silver clip in the form of a plumed eagle, c. 1935. The Brooklyn Museum, gift of William Spratling, accession no. 38.23.

which came to include gold, jasper, and jade. Always he rejected trivial decoration and sought instead an elegant simplicity.

A unique style gradually developed. Spratling pieces are easily recognizable, but because he was so influential in the development of the silver industry in Taxco there has also come to be a Taxco style of silvermaking in which elements of the Spratling style are used, although often without his elegance or quality of workmanship. The characteristics of the style are clean, modern lines; animal,

William Spratling, circular silver pin with serpent in relief, c. 1935. The Brooklyn Museum, gift of William Spratling, accession no. 38.24.

plant, and pre-Columbian motifs; and combinations of silver with semiprecious stones, wood, and tortoise shell.[15] The best silvermakers elsewhere in Mexico, in Oaxaca, Puebla, and Mérida, have kept away from the Taxco style, regarding it as deviant from traditional European-influenced Mexican silver.[16]

The apprentice system for training silversmiths almost universally used in Taxco began almost by accident with the teen-aged neighborhood boys who came to learn English and stayed on to help with the silver. It proved to be an excellent

William Spratling, solid silver
box, 1930s. Courtesy of
Sucesores de William Spratling.

way to train young silversmiths while producing quality hand-crafted silver at a
low cost. For the town it was a source of jobs and training for their young men.
Young boys started out as *zorritas* (little foxes) who ran errands but were also
expected to keep their eyes open, to watch and listen and learn. Spratling would
take any young boy who seemed eager for a trial period of a week. If the boy
showed aptitude and interest, he was kept on. If not, he was let go to make room
for someone else. Spratling did not give courses in technique, although he tried to
teach design and efficiency. His apprentices learned by problem-solving under the
watchful eye of a more experienced worker. He encouraged creativity by establishing an annual prize for the most original and best design, and he offered three
work days free of other labor for anyone who wanted to compete for the prize. The
prize was awarded on an annual Silver Day, a celebration of the founding of the

workshop, which became an important annual event in Taxco, with an elected queen and an evening ball.

Spratling was strict and sometimes impatient with his employees. He expected dedicated hard work and liked to see initiative and intelligence. No one dared to ask him twice how to do something, Antonio Castillo told me. Instead the young apprentice would go to one of the teachers who would say, "I don't know how to do it either. Let's try such and such."[17] The two teachers, Artemio Navarrete and Alfonso Mondragón, are remembered with great fondness by Spratling's first assistants, probably because they were the buffers between the gringo and his young employees, and Mondragón, in particular, is mentioned as an excellent silversmith.

In the early years Spratling often went with his workers on weekends to bars and dance halls in Iguala. He was interested in their participation in local festivals and dances, of which there were many in Taxco. One that particularly amused him was Mojiganga, a cross-dressing festival where men parade in women's clothing and dance in the streets.[18] An agnostic himself, he was critical of the Roman Catholic Church, which took the people's resources but left them in poverty, a subject he and Covarrubias often discussed, but when his workers arranged a special mass for Silver Day, he went with them. He bought his workers shirts and other gifts from Mexico City and New York. He liked to play jokes on both his employees and his friends with gadgets from joke shops such as a coffee cup with a lead bottom. "Have a cup of coffee," he would say and then laugh uproariously as his unsuspecting victim tried to lift the cup off the table. What the stories about Spratling often fail to convey is the twinkle in his eye, his quiet chuckle, the warmth of his manner, his charm, his integrity, and his intelligence. "Spratling was popular in Taxco," Carl Pappé told me, "because he was very smart, and the Mexicans like that."[19] "He was a man of culture, not just an adventurer," a local schoolteacher told me approvingly.

The workshop was paternalistic—of that there is no doubt. Spratling got rid of one North American woman who was socializing with his workers at late night parties by slyly hinting to her that there was a lot of syphilis around.[20] He liked to help his employees with housing, offering to design houses for them and loaning them money for down payments. Gobi Stromberg, an anthropologist who studied silver-making in Taxco, believes that Spratling's workshop fit the situation—a Spanish colonial town where the people were accustomed to a patrón.[21] It certainly fit the legacy of José de la Borda, the immensely rich miner who was everyone's boss and who gave the town what he thought it ought to have—a beautiful church, good roads (which helped in moving the silver), a good water supply, and Spanish-style red-tiled roofs for the miners' houses instead of their customary straw thatch.

Informal party at silver workshop, c. 1934. Private collection.

But paternalism was also part of Spratling's personality. He had, as he acknowledged when he saw himself in one of the characters in a Faulkner novel, an authoritarian way of taking care of people. He arranged people's lives with the best of intentions, if not always the best of results, Elizabeth Anderson admitted. The Spratling men, from the truncated memories young Bill had of them, seemed born to command. His grandfather Spratling had owned Oakbowery plantation, a cotton plantation in Alabama that before the Civil War had had 600 slaves. When Bill spent a summer there at the age of twelve, his grandfather was past eighty, "still a giant of a man who ran the place from his high porch overlooking the swept red clay of the yard. . . . " " 'Viola,' he would bellow, and from two fields away a little black girl would come running."[22]

Bill was befriended that summer by a middle-aged light-skinned black man, Blind Philip, a preacher, who was Viola's father. They went fishing and took long walks, and Philip told him stories about his father. "I loved Philip and suppose I sort of sat at his feet," Spratling told Gerald Kelly, who helped him with his autobiography. Philip told him the facts of life—no one else had—and one day he said, "I'se you' grandpappy's child."[23] One look at him, with his long jaw, thoughtful demeanor, and a nose like his grandfather's, and the young boy knew it was true.

Spratling's father, Dr. William P. Spratling, managed a different kind of community, the model sanitarium for epileptics, of which he became medical director in the 1890s after having written a classic text on epilepsy. Dr. Spratling selected the site in a bucolic area of western New York state, designed the buildings, and planned the daily schedules of the patients. It was a great advance in the treatment of epileptics, who usually before this had been classified with the mentally retarded. But it also reinforced in the mind of six-year-old Bill Spratling, Jr., the idea that manliness, especially Spratling manliness, had to do with being in charge of a community, with taking on responsibility and also taking for granted the right to make all the rules.

Managing a work force, however, inevitably produces headaches. Of the three aspects of running a silver business which are design, production, and marketing, production interested Spratling the least. He liked to turn it over to a deputy, while he concentrated on design and marketing.

Spratling was a very good designer but at marketing he was a genius. No one needs heavy silver bracelets or a silver teapot with a rosewood handle and a stylized silver jaguar figure as a knob. He had to create a market in a small Mexican town for these luxuries. He had to get would-be buyers into the shop and then to persuade them that the exclusive designs and the high quality of workmanship justified the high prices.

Spratling's targets beyond his friends from Mexico City were the tourists, drawn in increasing numbers by Taxco's growing reputation as a picturesque mountain town with a beautiful Baroque church. He got them into his shop by being highly visible as the legendary gringo expatriate in the town. Once inside the shop they were charmed by the association he made of his silver with indigenous Mexico. This was an expression of his own interests but also shrewd marketing, for it allied him with the muralist painters in Mexico City who were painting native peoples and with the tourist interest in Mexican archaeology and folk art. Spratling used prehispanic motifs in his designs. He exhibited pottery and objects from his archaeological collection in his showroom. On his desk in his office, where his most favored customers were allowed to go, he kept a collection of special pieces, including some archaeological erotica. He sold not only silver, but also tin lanterns, woolen serapes, and colonial furniture made of leather and wood, which allowed him to suggest that his silver—a high-quality luxury product of contemporary

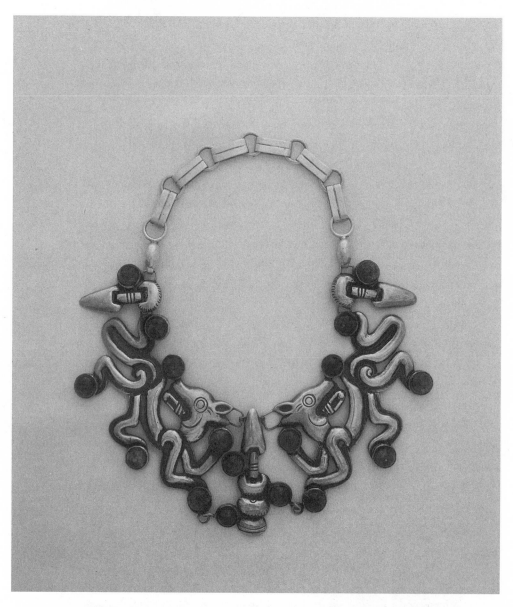

William Spratling, coyote necklace in amethyst and silver, c. 1944. Courtesy of Sucesores de William Spratling.

design that would have been at home on Fifth Avenue in New York—was a product of traditional Indian and colonial Mexico.

Spratling associated his silver with the natural world around him. He used local materials: silver from the mines that had made Taxco famous and quartz, amethyst, onyx, rosewood, and ebony, all of which were readily available in the mountains around Taxco or in the *tierra caliente,* and he liked to point out that these were the materials the indigenous people in the area had always used. Some of his designs reflected the local fauna and flora—a hummingbird necklace, a butterfly brooch, a much-copied dragonfly brooch. He kept several pet deer, a macaw and many smaller birds, some peccaries, and a pair of mazacoa snakes in his shop for his own amusement, but this also reinforced the impression that his silver was part of the local, natural world.

Spratling's belief in the creative possibilities of local craftsmen also helped to connect his silver to indigenous Mexico. The designs were his but not his alone. From his first days in Mexico when he was studying Spanish colonial architecture, he had been struck by the way Mexican artisans enriched European forms. They did not just copy European models, he said, but "gave the work physical vitality and dynamism, held in check by a feeling for equilibrium and sobriety." The result in art was "something new, something closer to the earth" than the forms brought from Europe.[24] He marveled at the way the builders and stone masons in Taxco adapted their constructions to the rocky terrain. Nothing was done according to preconceived forms. Everything was adapted to the site. Everywhere he looked he saw examples of remarkable ingenuity. In selling his silver he stressed that every piece was a combination of the designer's idea and the artisan's creativity and ingenuity in interpreting the sketch Spratling had given him. The buyer of a piece of Spratling silver got not only a Spratling design but also a bit of artisanship by the same creative, ingenious people who produced Mexican folk art and who had built the great archaeological monuments of Mexico.

And it was possible to observe these artisans at work in Spratling's workshop. Visitors could watch silversmiths hammering, tinsmiths cutting out designs, weavers at their looms, carpenters making the furniture, even a blacksmith pouring molten silver. Spratling had his own formula for the compound for sterling silver, preferring .980 silver rather than the usual .925 because it had a subtle glow and did not discolor as readily. He hired a skilled blacksmith to make this exact mix of silver and copper and had him pour out the molten silver where the tourists could watch.

It was important for Spratling's identification of his silver with traditional Mexican crafts that the silver was crafted by hand. He wrote in 1955:

Mexico today is the only country where . . . production by hand has never slackened. . . . Folk art here is an integral part of daily living—not simply an attempted revival of neglected arts. Only in Mexico will you find today the happily uninstructed little people, even in remote villages, busily producing new forms and giving virile and charming expressions to old needs. Their imagination is poured into the weaving of the simplest cotton textiles, home-spun woolens, intricate adaptations of traditional embroidery, good modern furniture, magnificent handblown glass, and, in perhaps the most flourishing hand industry today, the working of gold and silver.[25]

Sensibly however Spratling was not so committed to hand work that he would not allow machines when these made the work easier. He liked to quote René d'Harnoncourt as saying that a superior craftsman was "one who would recognize a superior instrument, or tool, and utilize it."[26]

Another side of Spratling's marketing was his insistence that his silver be a luxury product with a brand name. He had observed silver-making in Mexico City where silver was sold by weight which drove the quality down, except in the famous Platería Mendoza which had customers who recognized and demanded high quality and were willing to pay for it.[27] Spratling vowed to do likewise. He marked his silver pieces with a WS, based on the brand he used for his horses, wrapped each purchase in purple tissue paper, and charged high prices. Spratling silver became known for good-quality silver, high-quality workmanship, and originality of designs. He stressed to his workers the importance of the name. "Do you think that these fucking objects you are making can be sold like this? Why aren't you putting the stamp on them? What's valuable is the name," he would growl at an apprentice who brought him a finished piece he had forgotten to stamp.[28]

All of Spratling's goods were of high quality. His tin candlesticks, lanterns, and trays were better than average; his blankets were superb. We make the best blankets in Mexico, he would announce, striding through his shop, and knowledgeable buyers generally agreed with him.[29]

Selling was a game for him. He liked to pit his wiles against those of a customer. He admired Bernice Goodspeed, a North American woman who opened an art and crafts shop in Taxco across the plaza from his own and was a superb saleswoman. One of her tactics was to set a piece before the buyer and ask, "Does it speak to you?"[30] Spratling had others. "Aren't we saving that for Mrs. Morrow?" he would ask his clerk when he saw a customer eyeing an expensive piece. When an item did not sell, he raised the price, which usually worked.[31] Spratling sold his silver as fine art—the value of the piece is whatever people are willing to pay for it—and his margin was high. A bracelet that cost nine pesos of labor and three of silver would be sold for one hundred pesos.[32]

Stanley Marcus, who knew Spratling well and was no slouch himself as a salesman, told me that Spratling had a personality that was good for sales. He was engaging, gregarious, and always eager to meet interesting people, unlike Fred Davis, who also designed fine silver but who was shy and rather quiet.[33] Spratling presented himself modestly as an artisan, but he was the author of a book about Mexico and an authority on the folk customs and archaeology of the state of

Guerrero. In the right mood he would tell stories about his friendships with William Faulkner, Sherwood Anderson, and John Dos Passos in New Orleans or about Diego Rivera, Siqueiros, and other well-known contemporary Mexicans. Away from Taxco he spoke so eloquently about the glories of his adopted town that people came to visit and, of course, stopped at his shop.

61

He was a familiar figure in Taxco, striding across the square at the end of the day on his way to Bar Berta, either alone or with friends from Mexico City.[34] By 1935 he was already a legend and a tourist attraction. "Taxco would be quite another place without William Spratling. Nowadays, everyone who talks about Mexico is sure to mention him," Heath Bowman and Stirling Dickinson wrote in *Mexican Odyssey*. The two men from Chicago, a writer and a painter, spent six weeks in Taxco, staying with the Japanese painter Tamiji Kitagawa and spending most evenings at Doña Berta's. They drank "the John Dos Passos drink—tequila with lemonade" out of *copitas*, little silver cups that Bill Spratling had made, and watched him.

Perhaps this evening he has brought in a beautiful serving spoon, with a graceful rosewood handle, and asks everyone what he thinks of it. Only a few heretics ever object. He hangs his beaver-colored Texan *sombrero* on a hook and lights his stubby Acapulco cigar. There is a note to be sent, he or one of the others scribbles a message to someone in town and one of the little boys, always at the door, runs off to deliver it.

Or perhaps this is the day when he buys a *retablo* from the Mexican workman. There is a large crowd in the cantina, including several new arrivals. . . . The Mexican, hat in hand, enters almost apologetically and passes the *retablo* over . . . [an American woman shrieks about how can that be art and everyone is embarrassed]. [Silently] Spratling hands the man two *pesos*."[35]

By 1938 Spratling had almost a hundred artisans at work, including forty-six silvermakers. He was producing ten to twelve new designs a week, many of which were immediately copied in Taxco by a dozen small workshops which tried to compete with him by underselling him. Spratling took the worst offenders (including Serafín Moctezuma, whose initials upside-down looked like WS) to court, and they were duly charged and sentenced, but three years passed before any attempt was made to arrest them. By then they had all gone on to new designs and were friends again, so Spratling got the judge to rescind the order.[36]

Spratling's first museum exhibit in the United States came in 1937 when he was invited to participate in an exhibit at the Brooklyn Museum entitled "Contemporary Industrial and Handwrought Silver." Afterwards he gave a number of pieces to the museum.[37]

    Elizabeth Anderson started a business of her own in 1938. She designed color-ful casual clothes with Mexican-style embroidered decorations and hired local women who had been trained in embroidery by the nuns at a convent school in the town to make them for her. She still lived in an apartment in Spratling's house, down a long corridor lined with his collection of masks. Years later in a memoir she described their life together:

> Bill worked at his silver factory in the morning and we would meet for lunch at precisely one o'clock. We exchanged the news of the day and compared the male silversmith gossip with the female seamstress gossip and the disparity was astounding. Then we would go our separate ways. In the evenings I went to bed early, while Bill often had a small party with a group of men who played poker and had uproarious good times. The dirtiest of jokes were traded back and forth.[38]

"She was like an aunt, a relative," a friend from those days remembers. "She was the sort of woman no matter what was happening with his life, when he needed a friend, an elder, she was there."[39] Gloria Castillo, a North American who was married to the silver designer Jorge Castillo, remembers that Elizabeth Ander-son would drop whatever she was doing when Bill wanted something. He came in one day with yards of canvas, wanting her to make him a tent so he could go camping. Elizabeth Anderson was working on a rush order for Bloomingdale's of two hundred blouses, all hand-made and hand-embroidered, but she put that work aside to make the tent. She missed the deadline for her blouses, but she shrugged and said, "I can sell them elsewhere." And she did.[40]

    The two gringo entrepreneurs were occasionally harassed. The town authori-ties did nothing when a local madam moved her girls to a house directly across the street from Spratling and Anderson, despite their repeated complaints that the jukebox, screams, cursing, singing, and breaking of bottles went on until 3 or 4 every morning. Finally Spratling took action himself. He got some small capsules from his friend, Dr. Juan Meana, the physician with the local mining company, filled them with a foul-smelling concoction, and sent them across the street with a worker who pretended to be a customer. He and several of his apprentices watched from his garden as fumes rose across the street and several prominent local men fled the house cursing. Spratling was called to the municipal president's office the next morning, but no charges were filed, and the madam promptly moved to another part of town.[41]

Both Spratling and Anderson worked on literary projects. Anderson, who was herself a poet, translated fourteen sonnets by the seventeenth-century Mexican poet Sor Juana de la Cruz. Spratling had them published as a small pamphlet and one year sent it out as a Christmas card. He translated a book about Santa Anna's adventures but was never able to sell it to a publisher.

Spratling still did an occasional architectural project. In 1935 he renovated an old hacienda into the Hotel Rancho Telva for the Wells Fargo Company. The hotel was named for a famous opera singer who was married to one of the Wells Fargo officials. Spratling created a series of low buildings on at least six levels which seemed to flow down the steep mountainside. It was the first of the prestigious new hotels in the town, built to accommodate the ever-increasing numbers of visitors.

Spratling also worked behind the scenes to create the popular Bar Paco with its second-floor balcony looking out over the plaza. Not all visitors to Taxco were comfortable at Bar Berta, a simple cantina with a largely male clientele. In the late 1930s Spratling and Lois Cartwright Aguilar, a young widow from Kansas married to the manager of Spratling's workshop, decided to create a more congenial gathering place. They put up the money for Bar Paco, run by a man from Mexico City named Paco Arrendondo, and retained ownership anonymously for several years. They hired the artist and silver designer Hubert Harmon to paint murals on the walls.[42] These murals with their dancing donkeys are still in place fifty years later, and Paco's Bar has still the best view of the church and the plaza.

Among the visitors to Taxco in 1937 was Leon Trotsky. He and his wife were brought to the town by Diego Rivera and Frida Kahlo and lived for several months in a house across the street from the former convent of San Bernardino. Spratling is said to have made furniture for them.[43] There was much talk in Taxco about Trotsky being there, but few people saw him, for they lived, with good reason, a very secluded life in a house surrounded by armed guards. Trotsky was shot three years later in his house at Coyoacán on the outskirts of Mexico City.

For Spratling, professionally, these were satisfying years. His silver was winning international recognition, and money was flowing in, enough so that he could indulge himself with works of art, archaeological treasures, and a futuristic Studebaker designed by the well-known industrial designer Raymond Loewy. In New York for a visit to his dentist, he decided suddenly to ride to Frankfurt on the *Hindenburg*, the hot-air dirigible that soon afterward caught fire. His business had grown so fast that he had become the largest employer in the town.

Personally, however, his life was not so smooth, for Jenaro Díaz left him after several years to marry a local woman and take a job as bartender in one of the new Taxco tourist hotels. Spratling was so devastated when Díaz left that he contemplated suicide. "I tried to kill myself [by sitting in a car with the motor running], but the damned car wouldn't start," he told a friend.[44] Characteristically he turned his despair into the sort of anecdote he liked to tell, a wry joke on himself. If he could talk about it, perhaps the pain would go away. But however much he tried to joke about his feelings, his sense of loss was overwhelming, and loneliness became a somber note that reverberated through the remainder of his life. No one else ever took Jenaro's place. The strikingly handsome young Mexican who always dressed in black had been his *ayudante,* his trusted assistant, his companion on the road, the guard of his house, the caretaker of his horses, the focus of his affections. One small sign of how Jenaro Díaz's departure affected him is that thereafter William Spratling had no interest in horses.

CHAPTER FIVE

Trouble at the Workshop

In 1939 a new blow hit Bill Spratling, one that he as the unofficial patron of the town could scarcely have imagined. There was a strike in the Spratling workshop. The strike had no single cause. It was the combined result of accumulated grievances, a sudden economic downturn, and a prod from Mexico City.

Spratling contracted work out within his workshop, paying his workers by the piece, and buying from them only as much as he could sell. It was his version of Fred Davis's system of contracting out his silver pieces. He took responsibility for design and marketing but passed along the risks of production.[1] The system worked fairly well in the early years. Apprentices who were paid nine pesos for a bracelet could make six, seven, or eight bracelets a week at a time when fifty pesos a week was very good pay. But the apprentices knew that Spratling was selling each bracelet for a hundred pesos. In 1938 a newspaper clipping of an interview with Spratling was passed around and read in the shop, and it also led the workers to believe that Spratling was a rich man.[2]

Then in 1939 as World War II loomed, there was a sudden drop in tourism and in sales. The silversmiths had no work and no pay. At the same time President Cardenas was encouraging the formation of unions, and two union organizers came out from Mexico City to help unionize the Taxco silvermakers.

Spratling dug in his heels. He refused to sign a contract with the union and tried to carry on with "the Whites," as he called them, without the strikers, "the Reds."[3]

When the strike began, half of Spratling's workers, 72 out of 144, were participants. Gradually the number fell to 37. Antonio Castillo, a kindly and much-loved man in Taxco, was with the strikers. Then he read the union demands, which included items such as more bathrooms, and decided they were foolish. He went to Spratling secretly one night and apologized. Then he went to a union meeting, announced that he was going to go back to work for Spratling, and asked anyone who would go with him to step forward. One by one most of the men in the room did. Then with Spratling they worked out a compromise which involved a better system of pay. It was, for the moment, a good solution, and Castillo's actions earned him Spratling's life-long friendship and gratitude.

66   Later that year, however, Castillo and several other of Spratling's early apprentices decided to go on their own, some with the aid of North American women who had come to town and fallen in love with the young silvermakers. Spratling was not happy with this development, but there was nothing he could do about it. "The one thing I ask," he told them, "is that you not copy me."[4]

The slowdown in sales was only temporary. World War II brought great prosperity, as buyers from the finest stores in the United States started to arrive. With Europe closed to them, they needed luxury goods from elsewhere, and they turned to Mexico. What had been a local, retail market became almost overnight an export market worth millions of dollars. It was an astonishing transformation of one small impoverished Mexican town. Suddenly, everybody was rich. Not since Borda's lucky strike in the La Lajuela mine two hundred years before had there been such prosperity in the town,[5] and it was shared by everyone. Spratling liked to point out that the poorest silversmith in Taxco was making more money than the federal tax collector, the highest paid local official.[6]

A new influx of expatriates came in along with the foreign buyers, making Taxco an artists' and writers' enclave rather like that in Paris in the 1920s. The new hotels were filled with tourists. Natalie Scott expanded her business of renting out houses and gave almost nightly parties for the expatriates. Jane and Paul Bowles spent some months in Taxco in the summer of 1940 and again in 1941 when Paul had a grant from the Guggenheim Foundation. Jane liked it, but Paul found its mix of artists, writers, remittance men, and draft dodgers and its "carefully nurtured bohemian atmosphere" depressing.[7] The expatriates kept to themselves and spent much of their time drinking at Paco's Bar and giving masquerade parties. At least this was the Bowles's impression. Jane wrote part of her remarkable novel, *Two Serious Ladies,* in Taxco. Paul worked in a hut at the top of a cliff about an hour's ride by horseback outside the town, but he developed a serious case of hepatitis, and they left.

Eighteen-year-old Ned Rorem went to Taxco with his father in 1941 and was at first offended when a new acquaintance told him, "You know, in Taxco, nobody believes your father is your father." Rorem described the town as "so lewdly quaint" and, unlike Paul and Jane Bowles, felt there "an instant familial glow . . . the sense of everyone knowing everyone—the Spanish, the Mayans, and the loco Yankees who, were it not for the war, would be in Capri or Cannes . . . certainly there was suspicion, even hate, amongst the social and racial groups, but not inhibition."[8]

Rorem went to tea with Magda, a Spanish marquesa, and Gilberte, a French countess, two forty-year-old Europeans living out the war in Mexico and there met Paul and Jane Bowles. At Bill Spratling's silver shop he bought cruciform earrings for friends and silver brooches and silver egg cups for his mother and sister.

Rorem had been forewarned about sexual behavior in Taxco. "Everyone's available as long as you don't take them for granted; one tourist's head was cut off for having seduced a native, not because the native resented the act but because he resented being taken for a queer." In her memoirs, Elizabeth Anderson mentioned what may have been the same incident—an American was murdered with a machete and his body dumped in the *barrranca* between Spratling's and Natalie Scott's houses.[9]

Spratling increasingly pulled away from the expatriate community, some of whose antics he viewed with disgust. Taxco was his home, not his playground. "Bill rarely went to parties he did not give himself," Elizabeth Anderson recalled.[10] Gilberte Chartentenay, Ned Rorem's French countess who in 1994 was living in Cuernavaca, remembered the same thing. "Everyone would go to Paco's Bar in the morning and again at night, including Bill Spratling," she said. "But he stayed away from our parties and was rather aloof from the expatriate community. He concentrated on his work."[11]

In the heady atmosphere of Taxco in the late 1930s and early 1940s, Spratling spent money lavishly. He drove a big car, very fast. In Los Angeles for an exhibit of his silver at the Otis Art Institute, he bought a thirty-six-foot Seabird yawl and sailed it, solo most of the way, from Los Angeles to Acapulco. He built himself a beach house in Acapulco, a house on a cliff with a long terrace connecting the living quarters on either end.[12] Then in 1941 he bought a fifty-two-foot yacht (twin engine sloop) which he named *Pez de Plata* (the Silver Fish).

The *Pez de Plata* was a financial drain on him from the first to the last day he owned it. Three days after he bought the yacht, it caught fire and had to be completely rebuilt. Spratling used this as an excuse to make it uniquely his own. He knew that his friend Miguel Covarrubias needed money, so he offered him cash up front to paint murals on the renovated boat. Covarrubias's favorite model, a beautiful girl named Nieves Orozco, posed for the mermaid. Spratling posed, upside-down, for one of the male figures. The face of the sun was modeled on Mary Anita Loos, a friend of Spratling's.

The yacht required a constant crew of three and slept eleven. To justify the expense Spratling liked to invite his employees, past and present, to sail with him. He also frequently hosted large parties. As always, he served and drank a very fine Kentucky whisky and his own brand of coffee made from beans grown in Guerrero villages and roasted in a special way he had learned from a hundred-year-old woman.[13] One of his indulgences was silver plates and silverware, both at home and on his yacht. Antonio Castillo tells of the time Spratling found a basin of soapy water on the deck of his yacht left there by one of his workers who, mid-task, had found something else to do. Spratling kicked it off into the sea, unaware that it contained all the silverware. For the rest of the trip they made do with whatever cutlery they could find.[14]

In the early 1940s Spratling carried on a serious flirtation with Mary Anita Loos, the niece of Anita Loos, author of *Gentlemen Prefer Blondes,* whom he had known in New Orleans. Mary Anita Loos went to Taxco with her father in 1936 and looked up Spratling, as everyone did. She was tall, dark-haired, and very attractive, adventurous and fun, and interested in archaeology, which she had studied at Stanford. Spratling was immediately taken with her. He insisted on having her portrait painted by a local artist, and when she left, they promised to write to one another. Mary Anita Loos, setting off to travel by herself through Europe and Egypt, immediately wrote to him.

They saw one another several times over the next few years. Spratling visited Loos in New York where she had opened a public relations firm in 1940, and they went together to an opening at the Museum of Modern Art and made the rounds of restaurants, art galleries, and museums. When Spratling went to Los Angeles in 1941 for the exhibit of his silver at the Otis Art Institute, he stayed with Loos and her father at their Spanish-style hacienda in Santa Monica. He and Loos went shopping for supplies for his sailboat and for two Abyssinian cats he wanted to take home "to Elizabeth," and she saw him off at the pier as he headed off to Acapulco. He sent her postcards from small ports en route. One of them read, "This place is called Puerto Vallarta. Someday, someone will discover how beautiful it is."[15]

Twice in the early 1940s Loos accepted his invitations to visit Taxco. The first time she worked on a novel about Cortés and Malinche, and she and Spratling went about together—to Paco's Bar where they ate *chicharrones* and watched the life in the town square below, to Mexico City on his weekly visits to deliver silver, to Acapulco with Elizabeth Anderson and other friends for an expedition on his yacht, to the old chicken ranch he had bought outside town at Taxco-el-viejo where they swam naked (as was his rule) in a pool he had built. "We're Adam and Eve," she joked, but he turned the comment aside.

He was master of the unexpected and grand gesture. He came in one day while she was sitting sewing in Elizabeth Anderson's dress shop and dropped a gold brick into her lap. "What's this?" Loos asked him. "I've got thirteen of them, and thirteen's bad luck," he shrugged, "so this one is for you."[16] At night, when they played poker with friends at a ruined and orchid-strewn hacienda outside of town, he hired a mariachi band to serenade them. All Taxco gossiped about the new romance, but the two people involved did not know themselves what to make of it. Was the twinkle in his eye that implied they shared a secret for her alone, or did he do that with everyone, Loos wondered. She left Taxco with nothing explicit having passed between them, only to receive a short time later a telegram, "that was almost a proposal," begging her to return.

So she did. But Bill Spratling, having gone that far out on the limb of commitment, backed off. He was moody, there was an awkwardness between them that had not been there before, and finally he vanished altogether, moving out to his ranch for two days. When he reappeared, Loos announced that she was moving to the Rancho Telva Hotel. Spratling protested, but Loos felt she could not stay on at his house, nor even in Taxco, and she went back to Mexico City to stay with Miguel and Rosa Covarrubias.

Rosa Covarrubias was indignant that Spratling did not even stop by on his weekly trips to Mexico City, but Loos told her, "Rose, he's embarrassed. He went too far in inviting me to be in his life and then backed out, and he feels self-conscious."

When told about the telegram, Elizabeth Anderson had another explanation. "He must have been drunk," she said simply. "The boys must have had a few."

A year later when Loos was about to marry screenwriter Richard Sale, Spratling made a quick trip to Los Angeles to try to dissuade her. "Why are you getting married? Why don't you go to the Philippines with me on my yacht?"

He is incorrigible, she thought. It was not a proposal, just an idea for a pleasant vacation. "Bill, it's too late," she told him.

They remained friends, although years would pass between visits. But Spratling did not forget Mary Anita Loos. He owed her something, he seemed to feel, for asking and then withdrawing, for embarrassing her. Twenty years later, after his death, Mary Anita Loos Sale learned to her surprise that Spratling had written her, along with Elizabeth Anderson and his brother, into his will as his heirs.

Taxco was rich in the early 1940s, and Bill Spratling appeared to be the richest man in town. But appearances were deceptive, for in his enthusiasm Spratling overextended his business. By 1940 his shop was already losing money. Gradually over the next five years the unthinkable happened again as Spratling lost control of the company he had created.

As the new export market grew, Spratling incorporated his business to raise capital so that he could increase production. The name of the company was changed from Taller de las Delicias to Spratling y Artesanos. He sold three-fourths of the stock in the company to a group of fourteen partners which included twelve Mexicans and two North Americans. He started several new ventures, including a wholesale line of silver for the Montgomery Ward catalogue and a line of designs for silver-plated costume jewelry for Silson and Company in New York. Along with several other Taxco companies, he also made heavy silver ID bracelets for the United States military.

Finding himself behind on deliveries, Spratling hired ever more workers, but he had no room for them in his complex of buildings in the center of town. He had hoped that the fourteen partners, to whom he had sold a controlling interest in his stock, would help him arrange loans to finance the expansion of the company. When they did not do so, Spratling loaned 229,000 pesos (about $45,000) of his own money, acquired from the sale of his stock, to the company. With this capital he expanded the company in the spring of 1944 to La Florida, an abandoned hacienda near the arches at the northern entrance to the town. Spratling himself worked sixteen-hour days renovating the old hacienda, even helping to make the brick tiles for the roof.

The usual explanation for the boom in production and the prosperity in Taxco during World War II is that the silver workshops were producing luxury jewelry for the United States market and identification bracelets for the U.S. military. But a small study based on research done in 1980 but not published until 1997 on crafts in the state of Guerrero has revealed an unexpected new dimension in the Taxco story. The two researchers, Alba Guadalupe Mastache Flores and Elia Nora Morett Sánchez, interviewed silversmiths in Taxco, Iguala, and nearby centers of gold and silver-working. They were told about secret arrangements which dramatically changed silver production in these towns between 1943 and 1946.

The owner of a large workshop in Iguala told them he had been processing thirty kilos of silver a month, his designated allotment from the Bank of Mexico, turning it into silver beads, when in 1942 he was approached by middlemen who offered to get more silver for him. The silver would cost more than he was paying the Bank of Mexico, they said, but they would buy up all his production at a good rate. Soon they were bringing him 500 kilos of silver a month and giving him "fabulous" orders, for millions of chains, bracelets, and other objects. The workshop owner bought expensive machinery, presses, and laminators and smelters, for he could not begin to work that much silver by hand, and hired more workers. They were not trained silversmiths, but he soon discovered that did not matter. The buyers did not care about quality. They did not even care whether the silver beads they purchased were strung. They wanted jewelry which could be legally shipped across the border to the United States where it was melted down for the war production, including silver tubes, wire, and explosives.[17]

These secret arrangements help to account for the prosperity in Taxco during the later years of World War II, where "everywhere you went, up and down the streets, you heard the sound of workers pounding silver," as one of the expatriates

70

remembered.[18] When the war began, Taxco had around 300 silversmiths. Spratling's workshop was the largest, with perhaps 150, but there were eight or ten other workshops with at least ten employees each and other smaller ones. By 1943 Spratling y Artesanos alone employed more than 300 silversmiths. Other workshops had 150–200 employees, for a total of 1,200, a four-fold jump in the town within two years. Most of the new workers came from outside Taxco. They had been bricklayers or agricultural workers, and now with only the slightest amount of training were turned into silversmiths.[19]

Spratling's attitude toward these secret arrangements is not known but can be inferred from what happened in his workshop. He expanded enthusiastically in the early years of the war when the new export market opened up. He sold stock in his company to the fourteen partners, probably thinking that they would not dare to interfere with his management of the company he had created and hoping that they would help him raise money. The new partners, however, aware that Spratling was rich from the sale of his stock, waited for him to make a personal loan to the company, and eventually he did so. He used this money to finance the expansion to the new building on the outskirts of town. But Spratling y Artesanos continued to lose money. In 1943 his partners listened to the siren song of the easy money that could be made if they turned to machine production of silver jewelry, and they allowed a North American investor to make a large loan to the company for that purpose. When Spratling objected, they removed him from the business affairs of the company. In March of 1944 he was offered a contract to be managing director, a salaried employee, which, having little choice, he accepted.[20]

Spratling's objections are easy to understand. He could see, as could any forward-looking person, that when the war ended, the market for machine-produced jewelry would collapse, as indeed it did in 1946, when the trinkets they had been producing in such abundance could scarcely be given away. He had a long-term, not a short-term interest in Taxco which was his adopted home. He had built his reputation on the fact that his silver was hand-made, a high-quality product of Mexican artisans, not of machines. A bracelet made by hand was worth five times as much as a bracelet made by machine. Not just his fame but Taxco's rested on its reputation for skilled craftsmanship. After the war there would still be a market for high quality hand-crafted silver, especially that with a brand name. But there would not be much of a market for cheap silver trinkets mass-produced by the expensive machines, nor would there be jobs for the unskilled workers who ran them.

Spratling put the best face he could on the fact that he was no longer really in charge of his company. La Florida, the new workshop, opened grandly in June of 1944, by which time Spratling y Artesanos had 400 employees. He had a large bronze bell especially cast and mounted on the roof. The opening was celebrated with a banquet, and Spratling's employees presented him with a silver profile of himself made by the noted local silversmith Enrique Ledesma. The face he presented to the world was that of an entrepreneur at the height of his success. The actual silver profile made by Ledesma he did not much care for, so he hid it away in his house and eventually gave it to Antonio Castillo.

La Florida was intended to be a model workshop, Spratling explained to a reporter from the *Reader's Digest* who came to do a story on him. It was constructed on seven levels down the steep mountainside and had a cafeteria, soda fountain, and a swimming pool. It was supposed to function not only as a workshop, but also as a school, a club, and a community center. Spratling had thought about every detail, trying to work out in advance the problems of labor and management which had led to the strike five years before in las Delicias. Miguel Castillo Terán, who had stayed with Spratling when his brothers left to go on their own, was the administrator. The workshop was to be run by a committee, a junta of maestros, the master silversmiths. They were to elect an executive committee every six months and make the decisions about salary increases, holidays, and vacation schedules. They were even to hire and fire the cook and approve the menus in the cafeteria. This last provision was added after the men rejected the food in the cafeteria and chose instead to have their wives come and cook tortillas and beans for them on the street outside the workshop.[21]

Workers were divided into seven grades, from maestros down to trial apprentices who became craftsmen when they could make one simple object. Workers were to be promoted from grade to grade with corresponding pay raises only as their work passed the scrutiny of the maestros. Discipline was also handled by the committee. Spratling told the reporter for the *Reader's Digest*, "It is practically impossible to fire a man, under Mexican labor laws, after he has worked for you twenty-eight days, even if you catch him stealing; but if the workers catch him they have their own way of getting rid of him *pronto.*"[22]

Spratling's tenure as managing director lasted just one year. In March of 1945 he agreed to the humiliation of turning the day-by-day management of the company over to the man who had been his secretary. Spratling was named a director. In this capacity he tried to set up a revolving credit line for the company with a bank, only to have his plan rejected by the other directors. Eventually he learned that they had given the North American investor Russell Maguire, the owner of Meissmer Radio and Phonograph Company, entire control over the voting stock in the company in return for his investment of 200,000 pesos (about $42,000). In July of 1945 Spratling left in disgust. The heavy equipment which the new owner had brought in soon broke down, and no one knew how to repair it. When the war ended, the owner of the company sold silver, mostly to himself, at below cost. Within a year the company was bankrupt. The shares Spratling and the other directors held were worthless. Spratling lost not only the company he had created but also the money he had loaned it. He later charged that the destruction of his company was deliberate. Maguire had bought and intentionally lost money in "a whole stable" of small companies in Mexico in order to get himself into a lower United States tax bracket.[23]

A glowing article about William Spratling titled " 'Silver Bill', Practical Good Neighbor" appeared in the *Reader's Digest* in September 1945. In *Reader's Digest* prose, the author called Spratling "the most successful businessman I know," explaining he "has made a business out of his art and an art out of his business, and lives a dream life in a storybook town."[24]

But by the time the article appeared, the fairy-tale life it described no longer existed. Bill Spratling had left Taxco, the little town to which he had brought prosperity and international attention, and the company that had been the center of his life for fourteen years had collapsed.

CHAPTER SIX

RETREAT

His fall had been swift. In January of 1945 Spratling was "Mr. Taxco," the head of a company that employed 48 cabinet workers and 400 silversmiths and turned out wares for 140 foreign and 26 Mexican accounts. Six months later he was unemployed and had left town.

He moved to his ranch ten miles down the road at Taxco-el-viejo to nurse his wounds. The ranch was an old chicken farm of six acres he had bought several years before to accommodate one of his former apprentices, a man named Rafael Meléndez.[1] It was a narrow strip of land between the road and the river, screened from view by bougainvillea, bamboo, and tamarind trees. Beyond the river, a mountain loomed up, covered with small bushes. Spratling had built himself a small, very primitive house, little more than a camp, lit by kerosene lamps. The area was beautiful but desolate, which matched his mood.

He felt disgraced. His pride was hurt. He wanted to hide. He tried to leave the impression in Taxco that he was going on to bigger things, that he wanted to start craft centers elsewhere, in Mexico, in the United States, in Alaska. "My object, unspoken at the time, was simply to keep people in Taxco guessing as to whether Bill Spratling was stinking rich or whether he was in the gutter," he admitted later.[2] The truth was that he was broke and did not want anyone to know it.

Spratling's fall was particularly humiliating because it came just as many of his former apprentices were becoming wealthy. He had taught them how to be entrepreneurs. Now they were surpassing him, winning international acclaim for their designs, and managing large workshops. Antonio Pineda, one of Taxco's best silver designers, who had been an early apprentice in Spratling's workshop and later studied in Mexico City, had been invited to an international exposition in San Francisco in 1944 and subsequently had sold his entire exhibit of eighty silver objects to Gump's department store.[3] Héctor Aguilar and Los Castillos each had several hundred workmen, and there were dozens of other thriving workshops in the town.

Spratling settled in at his primitive ranch. He had immediately a couple of 75 flattering but inconclusive offers. The mayor of Zacatecas wanted to talk to him about starting a local industry there. More exciting was an invitation to come to Alaska as a consultant on how to develop native crafts.

The Alaska invitation came at the behest of his old friends and old Mexican hands, Ernest Gruening, now governor of the Territory of Alaska, and René d'Harnoncourt, chairman of the Arts and Crafts Board of the United States Department of the Interior. The idea was to provide winter employment for Eskimos and Indians in isolated villages throughout Alaska. They offered expenses but no salary, assuming, as most of his friends did, that Spratling was a wealthy man.

Spratling made a three-week trip to Alaska in September of 1945 and by October 1 had submitted a report to the Arts and Crafts Board of the Department of the Interior. He proposed an ambitious program: a central museum in Juneau and workshops/exhibit centers elsewhere in Alaska, each making its own unique products and staffed by older specialists and young apprentices on the Taxco model.[4]

Then for three years Spratling heard nothing more about it. The report seemingly dropped into a void. Spratling quietly vegetated, as he put it, in a rare letter to his sister Lucille.[5] The ranch is a world away from the lively town life in Taxco. He tried to get Elizabeth Anderson to join him at the ranch, but she refused, not wanting to live so isolated a life nor to give up her sewing business. She also realized that at the ranch she would become too dependent on him and too immersed in his life, which neither of them could stand. But they kept in close touch. A long-time friend of Elizabeth Anderson's who today lives in Cuernavaca said that for more than twenty years after he went to the ranch Spratling and Anderson spoke to one another on the phone at least once a day. Whoever got up first in the morning would call the other.[6] Spratling turned this, like so much else he did, into a game.

When he could not persuade Elizabeth Anderson to join him, Spratling invited his sister Lucille, who lived in New York, for a long visit in the winter of 1946–47. She came and stayed for several weeks. But for long stretches he was alone at the ranch, with only his cook, Manuel Quinto from nearby Taxco-el-viejo, for company during the day. He planted fruit trees: mangoes, oranges, guavas, tamarinds, and ten kinds of bananas. He had many pets, including a parrot, a deer, peccaries, otters, Abyssinian cats, and Great Danes. He studied medicinal plants growing wild on the ranch with the help of a nineteenth-century book by Maximino Martínez. One of his prize finds was a nut that was supposed to be good for hemorrhoids, which he delighted in sending to friends.[7]

Twice the quiet at the ranch was broken by invasions from Hollywood. John Ford and a film crew came to shoot some scenes for *The Fugitive* at the ranch. Warner Brothers came to make a movie short based on the *Reader's Digest* article,

"Silver Bill" but renamed "The Man from New Orleans" for Spratling hated being called Silver Bill and threatened to sue anyone who did so.[8] He refused to play himself in the movie but did agree to appear briefly at the end, a significant concession for him, for all his adult life he hated to be photographed. The movie short was bland but picturesque and showed all over the United States. At least one North American expatriate, Ted Wick, claims he moved to Taxco after he saw it. Spratling thought the movie was "vulgar" and "a typical success story," but he enjoyed the attention and the fan mail. "Half wanted to marry me, and the other half wanted a loan," he told an interviewer.[9]

Repeatedly he had to explain to friends and family that he was out of money, and the response was usually incredulity or bewilderment. His brother-in-law, Edward Bleier, a physician in New York, spoke for many when he wondered where all that money had gone. Not that it mattered, he assured Spratling, because he was confident that the latter could easily make it again.[10]

Perhaps bolstered by such sentiments, Spratling did start over at the ranch, building a new silver business. In 1947 he designed some new silver pieces and had them made in Mexico City. But beginning again was difficult. In the early 1930s he had wryly called himself "a button manufacturer" because one of his first products was silver buttons.[11] Now he was, he said, "an ex-successful button manufacturer."[12]

By early 1948 Spratling was so short of funds that he swallowed his pride and asked his old friend Elizabeth Morrow, the widow of the ambassador, for a loan of $7,000 while apologizing profusely for his circumstances.[13] He offered his house as collateral. Mrs. Morrow's bankers accepted his terms, but within a year the peso dropped so that the loan increased almost double in peso value.[14]

Around the time he was asking Mrs. Morrow for a loan, Spratling developed a passion for flying. It was a way, literally and metaphorically, out of the situation in which he was stuck. For five and a half months he averaged twenty-five hours of flying time per week.[15] He liked to claim it was an economy measure, that he could get better mileage in a plane than a jeep. But it was the adventure, the freedom, and, not least, a revived image of the swashbuckling adventurer that he loved.

In July the telephone rang at the ranch. It was Ernest Gruening, governor of Alaska, to announce that the Spratling Plan had been accepted and to invite Spratling to come to Alaska and direct the program. He was offered a year's salary and expenses.

It was the excuse he had been waiting for—a chance to leave town and an invitation to adventure. Spratling bought himself a two-seater airplane, an Ercoupe, which he named *El Niño* (the little one), and headed for Alaska on a daring solo flight. He took off from Iguala in late September, dipping his wing to the crowd that had come to see him off. Six hours later he landed in Mazatlán on the Pacific coast. The next day he flew through drizzle up the west coast of Mexico. He landed at Nogales and went through customs, announcing to general disbelief that he was on his way to Alaska. Heading north he got lost in the smog over Los Angeles, landed inadvertently in a squash farm near Eugene, Oregon, and went on to Seattle. He flew up the Inland Passage, finally landing near Juneau just behind the Mendenhall glacier. He had flown forty-five hours and sixteen minutes since he left Taxco.[16]

In Juneau Spratling met with Don Foster, the head of the Alaskan Native Affairs Department. They decided that several Eskimos (today Inuit) would be sent to Taxco to learn silver-making, their expenses to be underwritten by the veterans office. Spratling promised to provide 200 model designs, using Alaskan materials and motifs, which would travel throughout Alaska to stimulate local creativity. For these he was to be paid $10,000.[17]

From Juneau Spratling flew up through heavy rain to Cordova and then on to Fairbanks and the Arctic Circle through a mountain pass that was "a twisting wind tunnel." By the time he got to Fairbanks he had had enough. He left "El Niño" in a hangar and went on to Kotzebue and Nome overland.

Then it was time to return home, a flight made even more dangerous because winter was approaching. He now carried with him, in addition to maps and a sleeping bag, a raw polar bear skin as a souvenir and large chunks of Alaskan jade and ivory, which were raw materials for his designs.

Leaving Fairbanks the wind into which he was flying was so strong (69 mph) that he stopped to spend the night at an abandoned airport in the forest. Wolves howled all night long. "The wind was so terrific that I momentarily expected Niño to be torn loose from her triple moorings," he wrote in *Flying* magazine. "I was glad that the Canadians had insisted on full equipment—gun, food, rope, flashlights and the rest, including an axe."[18] The next morning, short of gas, he dropped down onto a gravel highway near a log cabin truck stop and taxied to the gasoline pumps, where he filled the Ercoupe with automobile gas and himself with pancakes, eggs, apple butter, sausages, and coffee—his first hot food in twenty-four hours.

But the worst was not over. A notoriously dangerous mountain pass lay in front of him. He tried to cross it three times but was driven back by the weather. Finally he took an alternate route of his own devising, trying to follow a railroad along the east wall of the pass, but it began to snow, great heavy flakes, and he had to lean out of the window to see anything. When a mountain cliff suddenly loomed up ahead of him, he "made a violent wingover to save my neck" and decided to turn back. Flying with his head out of the window, he could barely make out through the swirling snow the railroad tracks only twenty feet below his plane. But they were his life-line, as cliffs rose up on all sides of him, and he followed them out of the mountain pass back to Whitehouse. Juneau, on the Alaskan coast, was only an hour and a half away, but it took him five more days, making sometimes three tries a day, before the weather cleared enough to allow him to go that distance. "In the office [of Native Affairs] no one mentioned they thought I was crazy," Spratling wrote. "Only Customs called me in for a lecture."

Still he was only in Juneau, and he wanted to get back to Mexico. For six weeks he hung around Juneau, waiting for a particularly bad spell of rain to break. When it finally cleared, Spratling took off and headed south, but the winds were so strong he began to run out of gas. He headed west to Queen Charlotte Island, but it was fogged in, so he turned east and made an emergency landing at Fort Rupert on a concrete ramp that projected out into the bay. That daring maneuver made the front page of the local Fort Rupert paper the next day. He continued on, flying by instruments through thick fog until he reached Seattle. From there it was a long but uneventful trip of several days back to Taxco. He circled over the red roofs and green laurels of the town, dropped down to have a look from the air at his ranch, and then landed in nearby Iguala. In all he had logged 138 hours and 54 minutes in the air, flying solo.

Seven Eskimo veterans, Marley P. Lincoln, Joseph Wessup, Floyd Singyke, Tommy K. Lee, Frank Okpealuk, Francis Eben, and George Siparty, from six locations in Alaska, had arrived at the ranch at Taxco-el-viejo by mid-February.[19] Spratling hired three of his former employees, Luis Montes de Oca, Enrique Ledesma, and Alfonso Mondragón, to train them and asked his secretary to handle any problems. For the secretary this soon became a full-time job. Later he would say that it was impossible to believe how much scandal so few people could cause in one small town in so little time.[20] "They were all good boys, these Eskimos . . . ," Spratling reminisced later. "But it only took them a matter of days to establish credit in most of the *cantinas* and *bordellos* [in Taxco] and . . . they cut themselves a wide swath."[21] Antonio Castillo remembers one of them knocking off the large straw hat in which a baker's assistant carries rolls, so that the bread flew out all over the street. "They were very playful," he said.[22]

The Inuit men in turn were bemused by Taxco. They thought the hunting was rather a joke, so small were the prey, mostly rabbits and iguanas but also peccaries (small wild boars). They were impressed by the orange trees that grew at the Spratling ranch where they stayed but complained, ironically enough, about how cold it was in Mexico, especially at night. They could not digest well the local food, beans and tortillas, so Spratling made frequent flights to Acapulco to bring back fresh fish for them.[23]

80   While the maestros taught the men from Alaska silver-smithing at the ranch, Spratling worked on the 200 models he had promised. He used the ivory, chunks of jade, and baleen that he had brought back from Alaska, combining them with silver, gold, copper, wood, lapis lazuli, malachite, and abalone to make beautiful pieces—paperweights, letter openers, boxes, spoons, jewelry, flatware, candlesticks, goblets, bells, ashtrays. In some Spratling used what he liked to call Alaskan motifs, such as the North Star, the four winds, and animals. He was particularly proud of thirty-nine gold and ivory pieces, an unusual combination, and of a "Moby Dick" paperweight—a whale carved from ivory mounted on a piece of Alaskan jade to represent the sea.[24]

Ultimately, however, the project was not a success. "It takes five to eight years for someone to learn to be a good silversmith," Antonio Castillo explained. The Inuit were quick learners, but they were in Taxco for only two months. Spratling's original plan, to have Taxco silversmiths go to Alaska for six months, had long since been abandoned. Spratling's models were put on exhibit at the Department of the Interior in Washington, D.C., and eventually in Juneau and at the Mt. Edgecombe School in Sitka, but they never circulated in the interior of Alaska as originally intended. By October 1949 the project had shrunk to a plan for a technical training program at one location, the Mt. Edgecombe School in Sitka. Spratling was still willing to be the director of the program, but he wanted to have authority over design, production, and marketing, and he wanted the apprentices to be full-time workers needing to earn money to take home to their families, not students in a trade school working a few hours a week to earn semester credits, which he scorned.[25] Negotiations went on for months, but the project finally floundered for lack of funding. In 1952 Spratling appealed to Governor Gruening for permission to reproduce his 200 designs himself and sell them in Alaska, but the answer from legal counsel was that he could not.[26] Frustrated, he tried to get financing himself to set up a company in Alaska but finally gave up.

Spratling's disappointment at the outcome of the Alaska Project was twofold. He was proud of his workshop system which had trained a generation of silversmiths in Taxco and wanted to show it could work elsewhere. If he had been allowed to carry out his grand vision, Alaska might have been a success on a scale that would have made Taxco seem only a trial run. Also he was proud of his designs. It was intensely frustrating to have 200 designs, the results of months of effort on his part and some of his best work, lost because they could not be reproduced.

Yet the Alaska experience had its effect. Greta Pack, a well-known jewelry

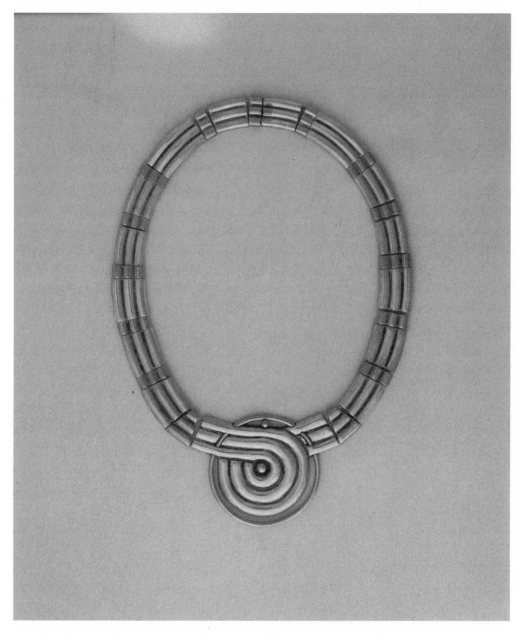

William Spratling, necklace of sterling and gold wash, Alaska period, c. 1949. Courtesy of Sucesores de William Spratling.

craftsman in the United States, got to know Spratling around 1950 while working with Mary Davis on a book on Mexican jewelry. In their book, *Mexican Jewelry*, published in 1963, Davis and Pack devoted a dozen pages to Spratling. Their comments represent their own judgment but also reflect what Spratling told them about himself.

"The experience in Alaska had a definite influence on the Spratling style," they write, noting that a number of his recent designs are based on "rhythms, lines, or motifs" with which he became familiar in Alaska. They continue:

> The earliest Spratling jewelry was simple in design, often using the motifs of ranches: ropes and straps and balls. Some were inspired by pre-Hispanic designs, and all were of heavy silver. The traditional designs have now disappeared and he is working for greater simplicity and a more refined line and as a consequence his designs have become more individual in character, more distinguished. . . . The Spratling designs are unmistakable among the thousands of pieces being turned out in Taxco. They have a clean, classic quality due to the absence of trivial decoration, and a fine feeling for the native materials which he uses in great variety.[27]

Davis and Pack note the combination of silver and tortoise shell, which Spratling had just begun to use, along with rosewood and also yellow jasper, which had recently been discovered in the mountains near Taxco.

Spratling's designs did change rather dramatically in the late 1940s and 1950s, becoming more sleek, more elegant, more international. It was a change he liked to attribute to his experiences in Alaska. But there is another possible influence— the presence in Mexico during World War II of a well-known French silver designer, Jean Puiforcat.

Jean Puiforcat was a third-generation member of a famous French silver-making family. His father, a collector of old French silver as well as an artisan and a good businessman, had transformed a small atelier into an internationally known firm famous for its high quality reproductions of fine seventeenth, eighteenth, and nineteenth-century French silver. But he encouraged his son, who was a sculptor and a friend of the architect Le Corbusier, to design modern pieces. Beginning in 1920 Jean Puiforcat designed elegantly simple pieces, carefully defining forms and volumes and eliminating superfluous decoration. He reintroduced the straight line, which had virtually disappeared from silver work, making angular and rectangular pieces. He combined silver with jade, aventurine, lapis lazuli, amber, amethyst, rock crystal, gray marble, ivory, and exotic woods such as ebony and rosewood, which Spratling was later to use. His work was exhibited regularly in France in the 1920s and 1930s in juried competitions, in the showrooms of the family firm, and in French design magazines.[28] It is possible that Spratling became acquainted with it in these years, although there is no evidence that he did.

But Spratling can hardly have missed Jean Puiforcat's work after the latter moved to Mexico, which he did in 1941. When France fell to Germany, Puiforcat

William Spratling, jaguar coffee pot in silver and ebony, 1950s. Courtesy of Sucesores de William Spratling.

William Spratling, silver champagne glass, 1950s. Courtesy of Sucesores de William Spratling.

William Spratling, necklace of sterling and tortoise shell, late 1950s. Courtesy of Sucesores de William Spratling.

and his wife, Marta Estevez, who was from a wealthy Cuban family, spent six months in Cuba and then went to Mexico. In 1942 Puiforcat established a silver workshop in Mexico City. Much of his work during the next three years was exported to the United States, where he had an exclusive contract with John Rubel on Fifth Avenue. In 1945 Puiforcat returned to France to settle some business affairs and died suddenly, two days after his arrival, at the age of forty-eight.

Not much is known about Puiforcat's activities in Mexico. One photograph shows him in San Miguel de Allende, a small town four hours north of Mexico City that, like Taxco, attracted many expatriates. There is no evidence that he and Spratling met nor that Spratling knew his work. But it is hard to imagine that Spratling did not. The circle of art and silver dealers in Mexico City was small. Spratling was sociable and curious, and he knew everyone. He made weekly trips to Mexico City. It seems almost impossible that someone did not introduce him to a famous French silver designer at work in Mexico City, or at least mention that

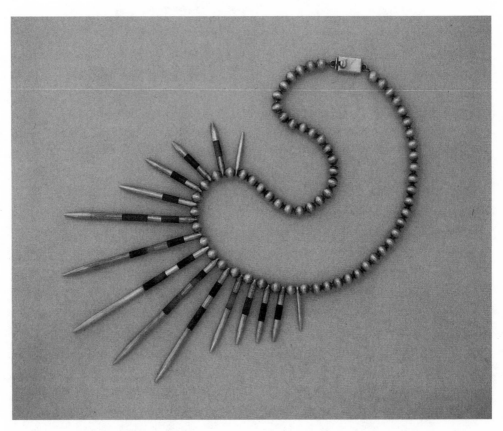

William Spratling, necklace of sterling and tortoise shell, c. 1950—55. Courtesy of Sucesores de William Spratling.

such a person existed, and Spratling would then have gone immediately to find out about him.

It is also evident that Spratling had from the late 1930s on some knowledge of the work of Georg Jensen and other Scandinavian designers. Georg Jensen pieces were included in the exhibit at the Brooklyn Museum in 1937 in which Spratling participated, and Mary Anita Loos von Saltza remembers a Scandinavian silver designer visiting Spratling while she was there.

In any case, whether through the influence of his Alaskan trips or of Jean Puiforcat or of Scandinavian designers or simply as a result of his own development, a significant change in Spratling's style is evident after 1947 when he again began to design silver pieces. Spratling himself said that a designer's unique style develops after months and sometimes many years of experiments.[29] At the ranch, where he had the leisure to concentrate on his designs, his style reached its full flowering.

As Spratling's pieces became more elegant, they were more expensive to make because they required more time and greater skill. For a brief time Spratling's designs were produced in Mexico City by a company named Conquistador owned

William Spratling, letter opener in silver and tortoise shell and silver and malachite and necklace, n.d. Courtesy of Sucesores de William Spratling.

by the Swedish industrialist Axel Wenner-Gren. But he was unhappy with the quality. In 1950 he founded a new company of his own, with a small workshop at the ranch. The company had a new name, William Spratling, S.A., and a new hallmark, WS written in script.

This time he knew what he was getting into. When he was asked to write a piece for *Artes de México,* a national art magazine, reflecting on his twenty-five years of silver-making, he was frank about the problems.

Silvermaking is not a simple business, he wrote. The artisans must be competent and dexterous, have "a spark of invention in their brains," and understand the possibilities of the material. The employer must be able to sort out their varying skills and deal with their personal problems. Meanwhile he or she must find designs that are unique and reflective of the place, satisfy all government regulations, and anticipate the demands of the public, trying to avoid either overreaching or underreaching economically. It is enough, Spratling wrote, "to dismay and cause gray hairs to any modern efficiency expert."[30]

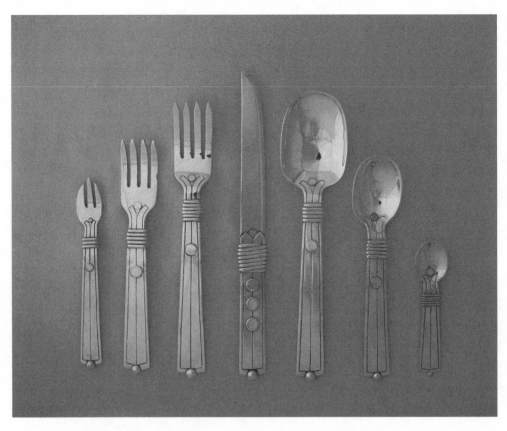

William Spratling, silver disk cutlery set, n.d. Courtesy of Sucesores de William Spratling.

Spratling compared a well-organized and responsible silver workshop to an architects' firm: there must be an idea man, a production man, and "a contact man," who is the salesman. In his own workshop he played all of these roles, but he looked wistfully at some of his former employees who had set up shop with extended families to help them—brothers, sons, wives, daughters, and sons-in-law. He especially admired Los Castillos, where Antonio, the head of the firm, was an excellent technician and production man while his brother Jorge was "the genius for ideas."[31]

Despite all the difficulties however, Spratling loved the local metal he had adopted. He wrote:

> The true color of silver is white, the same color as extreme heat and
> extreme cold. It is also the same color as the first food received by an infant,
> and it is the color of light. Its very malleability is an invitation to work it. It
> lends itself to the forming of objects in planes and in three dimensions of
> great desirability, objects to be done by hand in precious metal.[32]

William Spratling, bon bon dish in ebony and silver, late 1950s. Courtesy of Sucesores de William Spratling.

Spratling sold his silver in Acapulco, in a cooperative arrangement with the Castillos, Antonio Pineda, Héctor Aguilar, and others. He sold some in Taxco, in Héctor Aguilar's shop, the Taller Borda. He also opened a sales room at the ranch at Taxco-el-viejo. But he was off the main track. Buyers had to make a special trip to see him. Often they had already made their silver purchases in Taxco. He made arrangements with tour guides, as other silver workshops did, offering a percent of sales in return for bringing customers. But his silver business was never large nor even really profitable at the ranch. He had, however, become well known as a collector and dealer in archaeological pieces. People think the silver workshop supports the archaeology, he said, but in fact it is the other way around—the archaeology supports the silver.[33]

By the early 1950s Spratling's spirits had revived. He had begun a new silver business. He had developed the ranch into "a pleasant place to visit," as Stanley Marcus said,[34] with many varieties of fruit trees and tropical plants, a menagerie of

William Spratling, necklace in silver and green malachite, n.d. Courtesy of Sucesores de William Spratling.

animals, a silver workshop, and a growing collection of archaeological pieces. He had sold his yacht, the *Pez de Plata,* in 1949, but he had his airplane for adventure.

The stories about Spratling and his airplane are legion. He liked to buzz the homes of friends and drop out a roll of toilet paper as a signature gesture. He liked to torment his passengers, pretending that the plane was out of gas or that the controls were out of order. He would take his ever-present cigar out of his mouth and stick it up through a hole in the roof of the plane in flight to knock the ashes off.[35] He flew frequently to Mexico City to deliver silver orders and elsewhere on absurd errands, flying to Puebla to buy *camotes,* a famous Puebla candy, or to Acapulco to buy lobsters.[36] He was a daring, foolhardy flyer, and he loved to tell outrageous stories about his adventures—accounts of flying to Acapulco and other points on the coast, of landings on narrow beaches, of flying to mountain villages. The image he cultivated was one of carefree and fearless bravado. Behind the image was an invitation to fate to do with him what it would. He was not afraid of anything, one friend said, except a long lingering illness. Life was meant to be seized.[37]

The Ercoupe gave him a dashing image and also entry into the celebrity world which he loved. One of his adventures involved flying to Nassau for a society wedding in which he was to give the bride, Nancy Oakes, away. En route to Nassau he landed in Havana, Cuba, because he needed gas, and then, because it was getting dark, he made an emergency landing on Andros Island. Not until the next morning when he finally got to Nassau did he realize that he had been reported as missing on the international wire service: "William Spratling, millionaire, retired president of Taxco silver, has been lost at sea in his plane, flying from Nassau to Havana to the Oakes wedding."[38] Two Coast Guard destroyers from Miami, a search plane from Cuba, and two government seaplanes from Nassau had all been sent out to look for him. Notices of his demise, some of them outlined in black, appeared in newspapers from Alaska to Africa. He spent the next several weeks assuring his friends that he was still alive. The British rescue planes sent a large bill for the search to Lady Oakes, who had called them out.[39] Spratling enjoyed the excitement but was chagrined at the mistake, at the expense involved in the search, and at some of the labels, such as "Silver Tycoon" and "millionaire," that were applied to him.

The 1950s were the best years in Taxco, one local resident told me. The population was around 10,000, and in many ways it was still a small Mexican town. Pigs ran on the cobblestoned streets. Few people had telephones, so notes and invitations were carried around by servant girls or young boys. The high walls lining the narrow streets caused reverberations so that the air was filled with the sounds—of dogs, chickens, donkeys, church bells, the siren that marked the changing shifts in the mines. Tourists, however, had become the main source of income in the town, and some 200 North American expatriates had settled in Taxco. Among them were an occasional Hollywood or Broadway figure, but others were mining engineers or retired people drawn by the beauty of the town, the superb climate, and inexpensive living. They hung out around the town plaza, at Bar Berta, Paco's Bar, and the local hotels which made them a highly visible presence. The Mexican comedian Mario Moreno (Cantinflas) who played a Chaplinesque underdog, had a gag in one of his films that was greatly appreciated all over Mexico. He and a friend are discussing where to go for the weekend. "Let's go to Taxco," the friend suggests. But Cantinflas replies, "No. It would be foolish for us to go to Taxco as we cannot speak any English."[40]

Natalie Scott left Taxco to serve in the Red Cross during World War II but returned to carry on her hostess activities in the town and her interest in the local day nursery. When she died in 1957, the people of Taxco honored her with a grand

92 funeral. Among the mourners were the nursery school children, dressed in their best and carrying flowers. The teacher gathered them around the coffin. "Now cry," she said, and they did, wailing loudly and trying to outdo one another. "Now stop," the teacher said, and they were quiet. It became an often-told story such as Natalie Scott herself would have loved.[41]

Four years before, on June 27, 1953, Bill Spratling had been officially honored by the town of Taxco. On the sixteenth annual celebration of Silver Day he was named *Hijo Predilecto* (favorite son), and a short street near the house he still owned was renamed Calle Guillermo Spratling. A bust of Spratling and a plaque were placed nearby to mark the occasion.

Spratling was very touched. He was always emotional about public tributes. He would declare himself unworthy. The idea had been Ambassador Morrow's, he liked to say, for on an early visit to Taxco Morrow had remarked that it was a pity that the silver mined there had always been sent off to Spain and no silver industry developed in the town. Spratling would say that his success was due to the innate craftsmanship of his workmen and the ridiculously low price of silver. "I am no hero and no benefactor," he would insist. "My purpose in Taxco is just to make a living."[42] But at the same time he wanted to be appreciated, even to be loved. The tribute from the town was a gesture of acceptance and friendship as well as of appreciation for the material prosperity and the fame he had brought them.

But his pleasure at the honor was short-lived. The tribute was too much for small-town jealousies and long-nursed enmities. The bust of Spratling was repeatedly overturned during the night,[43] and there were attacks on him in the local newspapers. Taxco has five or six small and cheaply printed weekly newspapers, little more than scandal sheets, which in nearly every issue attack the municipal president or some other prominent local person. They are a means of venting jealousy and antagonism in this close-knit and competitive town. In 1953 two of the scandal sheets turned on Spratling. "Spratling is a Thief" one headline proclaimed, and the article charged him with stealing pre-Columbian treasures and smuggling them out of Mexico. The second accused him of seducing the young men of the community.[44] No one would have dared to make these charges publicly against Spratling when he was a major employer in the town, but now, absent and impecunious, he was fair game. And Spratling, who in earlier years might have been able to laugh it off, now could not.

Deeply hurt and shaken by some of the threats made against him—the father of one young boy threatened to kill Spratling if he ever showed his face in Taxco again—Spratling vowed never to return to the town. He spent the last fourteen years of his life ten miles down the road, slipping into Taxco only on a very few occasions, usually after dark, to see a few friends, and always leaving before dawn.[45]

A Passion for Archaeology

The charge that Spratling was smuggling pre-Columbian treasures out of Mexico brings us to his third career in Taxco—that of a collector and dealer in pre-Columbian art. It was a career he carried on from his first to his last days in Mexico, but rather more shadowy than his careers as a writer and as a silver designer. As collector Fred Field has observed, collecting pre-Columbian art was always regarded in Mexico as "an activity on the edge of legality, and a subjective issue depending on who you were and what connections you had."[1]

Spratling's first piece of ancient Mexican sculpture was the small stone face with a slanting jaw, the "pre-Hispanic Spratling," given him by Diego Rivera.[2] He immediately became interested in these small stone sculptures and began to collect them. On his travels through remote areas of Guerrero he bought more such stone "idols" and also clay figures from Indian campesinos who had uncovered them in working their fields. The "idols" were stone carvings unique to Guerrero. Most of them were small, from one and a half to five inches tall, and done in a severely abstract style, rather like Cycladic Greek figures or the statues on Easter Island except for their size. There were also animal effigies and small masks. Virtually nothing was known about these small figures, and Spratling was one of the first people to collect them.

Another source for these and other archaeological pieces was the market town of Iguala. Spratling would regularly make the rounds in Iguala, and he learned where to go for what he wanted. He would visit several selected stalls in the market, hunt up an itinerant photographer, and stop for a drink at a certain cantina. Years later he remembered, "In those days, Covarrubias, Rosa [Covarrubias], and Roberto Montenegro and I would frequently go down to Iguala and put in an entire morning. It was good hunting then, and we had to take along baskets which . . . we could fill up in the course of a couple of hours."[3] Many of the pieces of stone sculpture they bought were crude, but occasionally there would be a fine, highly polished piece, a genuine treasure. As it became known that he would buy these things, people began to come to him with their finds. He collected for himself. He swapped pieces with other collectors. And he marketed pieces, many of them to dealers and private buyers in the United States.

Spratling's exporting activities began early. In a letter in 1930 to a friend who worked for an art gallery in New York City, he wrote that he was sending the two best stone masks he had, via an intermediary, with four others to follow, if he had an opportunity to do so.[4] Within a year he was in trouble. He complained to the same friend of a series of disagreeable events which had left him in a bad state. He had been accused of selling a valuable mask for ten thousand dollars, of making excavations all over the state of Guerrero, and of exporting idols in trucks. Spratling had talked his way out of the charges, but the whole incident had frightened him and left him feeling betrayed by people he had thought were his friends.[5]

In his autobiography thirty-five years later Spratling gave more details about these same events. A local mining engineer had found, in a cave south of Taxco, an exceedingly rare Olmec mask of wood with jade incrustations. Spratling went to see it and tried to buy it, but the mining engineer told him he had a better offer from Chicago. Several days later Spratling went back to try again, this time commissioned to get it for a wealthy New York woman visiting Taxco. Since the mask had meanwhile been dropped and broken into many pieces by the mining engineer's cook, the mining engineer was happy to take Spratling's (and the New York woman's) offer of $500. A week later the fragments were smuggled aboard a boat at Veracruz.

But in Taxco, Spratling remembered, there was a great deal of gossip and there were exaggerated statements about his buying a jade mask for $5,000 and selling it for $50,000. He was called before the anthropological authorities in Mexico City, where he defended himself by producing a signed statement from the mining engineer that he was not the purchaser of the mask. Soon thereafter he gave to the city of Taxco "my then very small collection of artifacts." He added, "These pieces, including their glass cases, have long since disappeared, but the history of the mask still lives on, in various versions in the minds of many people."[6]

Reading between the lines of this account, it appears that a deal was made, that Spratling gave his then relatively small collection of pre-Hispanic antiquities to the town of Taxco in 1931 in return for the dismissal of the charges against him. He defended himself in his autobiography against the charge of profiting unduly from the sale of the artifacts. He did not deny that his activities helped move archaeological pieces out of the country, the more serious charge against him. He justified his activities by arguing that most private collections found their way eventually to museums and that museums would not exist without them. The wooden mask

94

did pass in 1949 into the collections of the American Museum of Natural History in New York. It remains one of the most famous pieces of Olmec art.

In these early years in Mexico when he was barely managing to eke out a living, Spratling offered for sale to friends in Mexico or in the United States whatever he could get his hands on: watercolors and paintings given him by Diego Rivera and David Siqueiros, stone masks and small figures from Guerrero, a collection of twenty old and rare Indian dance masks also from Guerrero. There are hints of a "Mexican manuscript" being available.[7] One long-time Taxco resident maintains that Spratling bought three heavy sixteenth-century silver candelabra from a boy whose father had been a church sacristan. During the revolution they had buried the candelabra. Later the young boy came to Spratling saying he wanted to sell

Wooden mask, Olmec style, from Canón de la Mano near Iguala. Courtesy of the Department of Library Services, American Museum of Natural History.

them so he would have money enough to move to Iguala. Spratling bought the candelabra for 50,000 pesos and sold them later to a North American. "He sold everything—fine stone, gold, jade," Carl Pappé told me. "The word gets around. 'I pay the highest prices. Come try me.'"[8] Another Taxco resident said that Spratling financed the expansion of his workshop into La Aduana in 1934 through the sale of two archaeological pieces, very rare gold figurines, that he had found.[9] When he could not sell a piece because it was too well known or too large to be smuggled out of the country, he would trade it with a Mexican collector for something he could sell. A great deal of bartering, "horse-trading" as Spratling liked to call it, went on between the small group of collectors and dealers who all knew one another. Yale archaeologist Michael D. Coe has traced the history of one exceptional object, a blue-green jadeite Olmec bust of a woman, which was acquired by Spratling, probably in Iguala, then sold to Covarrubias who in turn sold it to the collector and surrealist painter Wolfgang Paalen, who traded it back to Spratling, who sold it again. The bust passed through the hands of yet another owner before being acquired by a New York dealer who sold it for $4,000 in 1948 to Robert Woods Bliss, the founder of the Dumbarton Oaks Collection where it rests today.[10]

To understand Spratling's attitude (and his actions), it is necessary to place them in the context of the Mexican situation in the 1930s and afterward. A Mexican law dating from 1897 declared that all archaeological monuments were the property of the nation and forbade the export of movable objects without official permission. But "official permission," when anyone bothered with it, was usually easy to obtain. Many of the archaeological sites in Guerrero, including some registered on maps, were difficult to get to and to guard. As Daniel Rubín de la Borbolla, a friend of Spratling's and eventually director of the National Museum of Anthropology, wrote, the situation "gave rise to a certain official tolerance [of plundering of sites] and in some cases a profitable association between the diggers and local authorities."[11] Under these circumstances Spratling could convince himself that if he did not do it, someone else would, that he was simply taking advantage of a state of affairs before the police themselves or customs officials did so. It became a game to see who could get there first and deal most shrewdly, the sort of a game that he loved.

Spratling's collecting of archaeological pieces may have come to a temporary halt in 1931, but not for long.

In 1935 rumors began to circulate among the handful of people interested in pre-Columbian objects that a brickyard on the northwest outskirts of Mexico City was yielding treasures. Miguel Covarrubias, Diego Rivera, and Bill Spratling went there immediately. They found that the workmen digging there for clay to make bricks had to separate out potsherds, figurines, and other archaeological remains before they could use the clay. The three friends urged the diggers to stop lest they damage the figurines, but the workmen said they had been hired to dig the clay and needed the money. So Spratling, Covarrubias, and Rivera offered to pay them one centavo for each piece they saved. Three days later, when they finally left, they had run out of money, but they had boxes and boxes of clay figurines.[12] Covarrubias named the site Tlatilco after the Indian village nearby, a Nahuatl word which means "place of mounds" or "where things are hidden,"[13] and a visit there became a routine Sunday outing. "Going to Tlatilco with a pocketful of change and returning with an archaeological puzzle or with an artistic surprise became our weekly habit," Covarrubias wrote.[14] They found unusual pots. They found clay seals which are flat and cylindrical stamps used to print designs on textiles, pottery, and human skin. By 1937 Spratling had a collection of 119 clay seals, and he sent photostats of the designs to Franz Blom, archaeologist at Tulane whom he had gotten to know well during his New Orleans years.[15] They found more clay figures, some daubed with red, yellow, and white paint which showed how the people had used the seals to paint decorations on their bodies.

The clay figures, which came be called "pretty ladies," were in a primitive or "Archaic" style and were charming. The vast majority were representations of women, but there were also warriors, children, ball players, and priests. They were "modeled with a directness and feeling for form that was later lost when the arts became more formalized," Covarrubias felt. They were "simple and unassuming, but gay and sensitive, free of all religious academism."[16] To Spratling, Covarrubias, and Rivera, all of whom disliked organized religion, they seemed to indicate a joyous, humanistic culture, one concerned with life in the here and now, not with gods and goddesses.

The clay figures at Tlaltilco were remarkable enough, but there were also carvings in stone, including jade necklaces, and some pottery in a related style, made by people technologically more skilled and artistically more sophisticated than the makers of the small clay figures. Covarrubias was particularly pleased with two figures which he bought from the brick makers. One was of clay covered with white slip, the other was of polished dark green serpentine stone, but both of them were in a style different from the clay figures and different from the classic cultures of Mexico—Aztec, Maya, Toltec, Zapotec. Covarrubias thought them similar in style to the colossal basalt stone heads and small jade carvings recently found near Veracruz, which had been named "Olmec" after the legendary ancient culture on the Gulf coast. What particularly interested him was that these Olmec figures were found alongside much cruder "Archaic" figures, seeming to indicate that two different peoples had co-existed here at some very early date. Had the Olmecs with their more highly developed culture moved in from their place of origin elsewhere in Mexico?

As Tlatilco became known, other collectors hurried there. The brickmakers soon found it far more profitable to dig for treasures than to make bricks, and looters joined them. Covarrubias became so upset at the wanton destruction of the site that he took to guarding it himself at night. In 1942 he asked the Institute of Anthropology to launch an official exploration of the brickyards. This was done, Covarrubias was appointed director, and the looting was stopped, at least in the area under the control of the institute where only authorized personnel were allowed. Serious archaeological work at the site, begun then, continued into the 1970s. It showed the site to have had intensive human occupation in the remote past (200 B.C. to A.D. 200) and later with Carbon 14 dating perhaps as early as 1450 B.C.[17]

The Tlatilco brickyard turned Miguel Covarrubias into a passionate researcher in archaeology.[18] Spratling and Diego Rivera were mainly interested in aesthetics, in the design and form of a piece and the skill with which it was made. Covarrubias was interested in aesthetics, too, and of the three he had the best eye, the best educated and at the same time intuitive sense of whether a piece was good or not. But Covarrubias also wanted to know its history and context and on the basis of these began to make far-reaching hypotheses about the progression of civilizations in ancient Mexico. Meanwhile, he, Spratling, and Rivera competed in a friendly rivalry as they built up their three great collections of pre-Hispanic antiquities.

They were an impressive triumvirate. Diego Rivera was a Gargantuan man and a man of Gargantuan appetites: for art, for women, for food, for work, for political arguments. Elizabeth Anderson did not like him, for she thought he was totally self-involved. Spratling enjoyed him and admired him but did not completely trust him. Whenever Diego was around, Spratling would ask his secretary to keep an eye on him, for Diego was prone simply to pocket any piece of jewelry or archaeological object that caught his fancy.[19]

Miguel Covarrubias, on the other hand, was remarkable for his sweetness of character as well as his overflowing and perceptive creativity, and Spratling soon came to regard him as his best friend. Like Spratling, Covarrubias was a writer and an artist, and they both had made ethnographic-like explorations into other cultures. Spratling had immersed himself in rural Mexico. Covarrubias had explored New York City and then moved on to Bali and finally the Isthmus of Tehuantepec in southern Mexico. He published his impressions in two books of caricatures, *The Prince of Wales and Other Famous Americans* and *Negro Drawings* (about Harlem) and in two nonfiction books, *Island of Bali* (1937) and *Mexico South*

Miguel Covarrubias, Nicholas Murray, and William Spratling. Photo courtesy of Alfonso Soto Soria.

(1946). When Covarrubias became passionately interested in the Olmec (he called it his "obsession"),[20] he approached it in the same spirit of cultural inquiry. It was a civilization he was determined to learn more about, not simply a style he admired and wanted to collect. He turned himself into an archaeologist, working first at Tlatilco and then under the direction of Smithsonian archaeologist Matthew Stirling at recently discovered Olmec sites in Veracruz and Tabasco. In 1942 he argued at a Round Table conference in Tuxtla Gutierrez that the Olmecs were the earliest civilization in Mexico, the "mother culture" from which the others had come. It was a controversial hypothesis that was derided at the time by the leading archaeologists but has since come to be widely accepted.

In deference to Covarrubias's "obsession," Spratling and Rivera decided not to compete with him, although they too loved Olmec art. After Tlatilco Rivera concentrated on the west coast of Mexico, especially the remarkable ceramic animal figures and pots coming from burial sites in Colima, Nayarit, and Jalisco. Spratling, having collected a large number of clay seals and clay figures from Tlatilco, went back to his original interest, the archaeology of the state of Guerrero, and again began to accumulate the small, very schematic and stylized masks, figures, temple facades, and representations of animals such as jaguars, frogs, snakes, monkeys, and parrots carved mostly in a hard green stone which turned up so frequently around Taxco and along the Balsas River. Spratling made a significant collection of this art which is among the most abstract of all pre-Columbian styles. In 1944 Covarrubias named the style Mezcala, the name for the middle Balsas River along which they were found. He thought the style was early, perhaps A.D. 600.[21] Other experts have suggested that it was late, perhaps A.D. 1300. No one knows because, despite the fact that experts estimate some 20,000–25,000 pieces of Mezcala art have passed into public and private collections, there has not yet been a systematic excavation of a Mezcala site.[22] Without associated organic material, Carbon 14 dating is impossible. With no knowledge of the context and the stratigraphic level in which the pieces were found, it is impossible to relate Mezcala to any other known society. All that can be said is that the objects look like one another and that they seem to be a purely local style.

One of Spratling's best sources for Mezcala art as well as ceramic pieces in other styles was a woman junk dealer in Iguala who with her family has become legendary among collectors in Guerrero. Spratling met her in 1938 when she was a young woman, eighteen years old, illiterate but street smart and spunky, and married to a handsome deaf and mute man. From a serape spread out on the ground on which were piled old bottles, rusty tools, and a few "idols" dug up by farmers in their fields, the couple built an empire which came to include a dozen houses and small businesses in Iguala, managed in theory by one or another of their twelve progeny but overseen in fact by their formidable mother. In his autobiography Spratling called her "an extraordinary woman" who would have made a great revolutionary general,[23] implying at the same time the not necessarily contradictory opinion that she was an ingenuous and very clever rogue. When he and Covarrubias and other collectors began to come to her, looking for antiquities, she grasped immediately what they wanted, figured out how to supply it, and became shrewdly knowledgeable about what she was selling. By the 1960s she was said to have sources for antiquities in at least 200 villages and clients from all over Mexico, including cabinet ministers, supreme court justices, and movie actors, to whom she would sell for her "normal" profit of one to two thousand percent.[24] Vigorous, uninhibited, lusty, she intimidated the police with her harangues and then used the police in turn to intimidate the campesinos, usually landless farm workers, who sold to her. This she could do because buying and selling antiquities was legal (until 1973, when a new law was passed), whereas digging or exporting without a permit was not legal. It all became a matter of definitions, bribes, threats, and arm-twisting.

In January of 1995 I went to visit her. Her name is Feliz Gutiérrez de Salgado, and her husband, who died in 1993, was Manuel Batilo, but she is widely known as

Greenstone celt figure, Pre-Columbian, Mezcala. The Art Museum, Princeton University.

La Muda (meaning the wife of the deaf man who was El Mudo), and it was by asking around in the gold market in Iguala for the family of El Mudo that I was eventually given directions to a hardware store on Bandera National Street run by one of her sons. She lives in a house that opens directly off the street about five blocks from the center of Iguala, a street so noisy with passing trucks that we shouted most of our conversation at one another. A tiny, gray-haired but still vigorous woman at seventy-five, she was energetically sweeping the floor when I arrived. She handed the broom to a granddaughter, welcomed me warmly ("Don Guillermo, si!"), and ushered me to a coverlet-covered bed arranged along the wall in the front room. "Don Guillermo and I were great friends," she told me and proudly pointed out the photograph of herself on the wall that he had taken. The photograph is striking. She must have been about thirty years old at the time, with dark hair, flashing eyes, and head held high. She looked like a *soldadera*.

We looked at other photographs, including several family groupings and autographed photos of movie stars. She was eighteen years old and selling junk "to artists" in the plaza in Iguala when they met, she said. Don Guillermo liked to buy spurs and other horse things, and he gave her money to buy *dioses* (gods). Yes, he bought a lot from her but also from many other people. She was not much interested in talking about her business. He called her "Chica," she remembered. He came often and sometimes would stay to eat with them, especially if there were chiles rellenos, but he was always in a hurry. He was energetic and "*delgado, como yo* [thin, like me]," she grinned. She did a vigorous imitation of a cockfight, to demonstrate how "energetic" they both were, and an imitation of herself standing solemnly alongside Spratling's casket as a part of the honor guard before his funeral, both half-serious, half-wry self portraits. She was warm, curious, and open but not prying, quick, savvy, independent, and outspoken, and everything she said or did was underlined by an immense dignity. I could understand why Spratling had liked her—this tiny, illiterate Mexican woman was in many ways a female version of himself.

Suddenly she remembered. Did I like mezcal? She spoke a few words to her granddaughter who left the room and returned a few minutes later with a dusty brown bottle and two small glasses. Thirty years ago Spratling had given her a bottle of his special aged Guerrero mezcal with his own label. Grinning, she pointed to the label. "Fine Old Sour Puss Mezcal" it read, beneath a photograph of a portrait bust of him done by Helen Escobedo, a Mexico City sculptor. She poured me a small amount but took only a drop herself, and I noticed that the bottle was still two-thirds full. Had she treasured it all these years, I wondered, or had she, the old rogue, perhaps refilled it? As I left, she pressed a parting gift into my hands, a pair of rusty spurs.

"Fine Old Sourpuss" mezcal label with photo of sculpture of Spratling by Helen Escobedo. Courtesy of the sculptor.

Fine Old Sourpuss

★ ★

SPECIAL RESERVE

OLD SOURPUSS. por HELEN ESCOBEDO

LEGITIMO MEZCAL AÑEJO DE LA SIERRA MADRE DE GUERRERO
embotellado por
CASA SPRATLING

Spratling's friendship and his dealings with Feliz Gutiérrez de Salgado spanned nearly thirty years. He was godfather to her daughter Betty. He took on her eldest son as a trial apprentice in silver-making, although that experiment lasted only a few weeks. She telephoned Spratling, sometimes several times a week, when she thought she had something he might like or would come herself to the ranch. Spratling would lick the pieces she brought, his secretary Margarita González Banda said, to see if they were authentic.

Spratling's enthusiasm for the art of Guerrero, especially the stone sculptures in the Mezcala style, was contagious, and he helped several other residents of Taxco make collections of their own. A North American orthodontist, Dr. Milton Arno Leof, his wife Tiby, and dental technician Daniel Brenman lived in Taxco in the late 1940s and early 1950s and together amassed a large collection. They often went out with Spratling in his airplane, landing near small villages where they inquired about "idols." They became experts in technical analysis of the objects, especially the methods used in carving, which became important as the number of faked objects increased.[25] Spratling also befriended a young couple, Josué Sáenz, the banker son of Moisés Sáenz, and his wife Jacqueline, who were collectors of pre-Columbian art. Spratling introduced them to Covarrubias and took them around Guerrero in his small plane. They went to "dozens" of inaccessible zones of the state, Jacqueline Sáenz later wrote. "People in the area where we landed came out from their corn patches to sell their chance finds." But such arduous methods were only necessary if one wanted the finest pieces. In the markets in Taxco and Iguala merchants hawked carved and polished stones "as if they were tomatoes. . . . Even along the highway between Iguala and Chilpancingo they had their straw mats full of sculptures of clay and stone."[26]

In 1952 Spratling added a third specialty to his archaeological collections, in addition to the clay objects from Tlatilco and the Mezcala stone sculptures, when he learned about some unusual pottery objects that were coming from near Veracruz around the village of Remojadas. They were human figures, usually from six to twenty inches tall, made of red clay and painted with red, white, and yellow earth and with black resin. Many had smiling faces and elaborate headdresses. Before 1952 the few known examples were usually labeled Totonac, but suddenly the market was flooded with these smiling heads, which came to be called the Smiling Face complex or Remojadas figures. Collectors who wanted only rare pieces disdained them, but Spratling was charmed by them and kept buying. In 1959 he gave 189 Remojadas objects to the new museum at the National Autonomous University of Mexico where his friend Daniel Rubín de la Borbolla was director. The university published a book on his collection with a brief text by Spratling and photographs by Manuel Alvarez Bravo.

To Spratling the smiling faces seemed to represent a sheer delight in living. He titled the book *More Human than Divine* and liked to think that he had again found a humanistic culture such as he, Covarrubias, and Rivera were always looking for, where people quietly celebrated their sense of plenitude and their joy in being alive, rather than being obsessed with sacrifices to the gods. More recently scholars have suggested that the so-called smiling faces with their hard, wide grins might be depicting drug-induced trance states.[27]

Spratling dedicated *More Human than Divine* to Miguel Covarrubias, who had died three years before, in 1957, of a perforated ulcer, at the age of fifty-three. Covarrubias's death was a blow to Spratling so severe that he never really recovered from it. Covarrubias was the person he considered his best friend, the person whose company he most enjoyed. In his last years, Spratling lost some of his geniality, becoming more isolated, lonely, and cantankerous, even bitter, a progression that seems to have begun with Covarrubias's death. About Covarrubias's former wife, Rosa, he was especially bitter, and with some reason, for Rosa Covarrubias had made her former husband's last years miserable after he took up with a young dancer. "I can't stand to breathe the same air as that bitch," Spratling was heard to say about Rosa Covarrubias, abruptly leaving a party after he learned she was there.[28]

In one way Covarrubias's death set Spratling free. He could keep the Olmec objects he previously had passed along to his friend, and he immediately began to do so. Of his collection and the little museum he eventually built for it, Spratling later said wryly, "Miguel Covarrubias would have loved it, only he would have never left me in peace until we had, one by one, concluded a swap on much of the material."[29]

Now as he began to collect Olmec art, Spratling became fascinated by jade, especially the exquisite bluish-green translucent jadeite used in the finest Olmec carvings and regarded by pre-Columbian peoples as more precious than gold or silver. Collecting jade, looking for a source or sources of this jade in Guerrero where he believed it must have come from, designing special pieces of jewelry using jade beads or pendants in combination with silver or gold, and planning a book on "Jade in America"—all of these occupied him in the years after Covarrubias's death.[30] There were rumors in the 1960s that Spratling had found a source of the blue-green jadeite in Guerrero and was using it in his workshop, but the location of that source, if it exists, remains a secret.[31]

This new interest in Olmec art and in jade was, however, small compensation to Spratling for the loss he experienced with Covarrubias's death. Covarrubias was not only his friend. He was also the authority with the almost unerring eye who had verified the archaeological pieces Spratling admired and collected and sold.

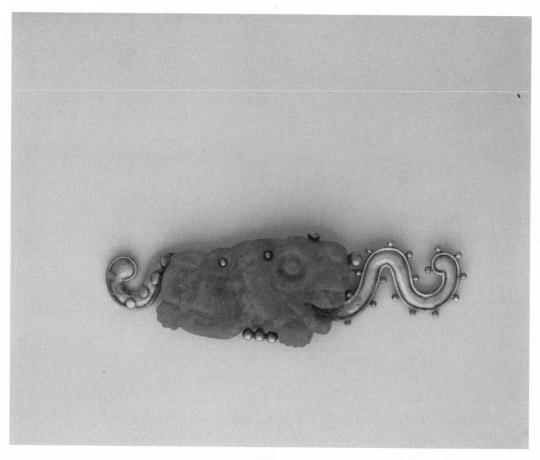

William Spratling, brooch of pre-Columbian jade and gold, early 1950s. Courtesy of Sucesores de William Spratling.

Without Covarrubias to consult, Spratling was no longer sure whether a piece was authentic or not. He began to pretend it did not matter. He began to play games, testing to see what he could put over on a supposed expert. His last years were marred by suspicions and accusations that he was collecting and selling fakes.

When Spratling began his collecting, so few people were interested in pre-Columbian antiquities, especially the little-known styles from the state of Guerrero, that the price was low. There was no incentive to produce fakes. But as the number of collectors increased, prices rose. Visitors to Taxco increasingly wanted to buy not only silver but also antiquities, and local dealers were quick to accommodate them.

A community of stone workers had grown up at Pedro Martín on the outskirts of Taxco to supply the silvermakers with semiprecious stones for their jewelry. Many of these stone workers were highly skilled, and several families of them began to specialize in making reproductions or "interpretations" of archaeological pieces. Inevitably some of these copies began to be passed off to unwitting buyers as authentic examples of pre-Columbian sculpture.

As early as 1952 a young American anthropologist named Frederick A. Peterson warned that many of the stone masks, plaques, and statuettes sold in Taxco were fakes. He knew at least five families in and around Taxco who worked at making these artifacts, he wrote in a Mexican anthropology journal, and he estimated that at least 5,000 objects had been made over the past twenty years, "so marvelously finished, cracked, abused, and aged" that they deceived the experts and could be found in museums and private collections around the world.[32] Peterson suggested some telltale features: was the surface not sufficiently weathered, were the eyes carelessly done, was the nose too wide, were the eyebrows too deep, was an instrument mark not polished away? But these criteria were ephemeral, for the stone-workers themselves were likely to be among the first to read his warning, and they would immediately stop making these errors.

The scenario for selling these pieces was predictably ingenious. The shops were full of crude pieces intended for tourists. When a collector walked in, he was shown these. If he protested that these were only cheap reproductions, the dealer said, "Ah, señor, I see that you are an expert. I will not try to fool you. Now I will show you some authentic pieces."[33] The high-quality reproductions would then be produced. "Here, now you can see for yourself the difference between the false and the authentic." Or a dealer might buy several pieces and then hire a local farmer to dig them up, perhaps after inviting a potential buyer to come and watch the "excavation."

Ezekiel Tapia, a much-admired sculptor in Taxco who comes from a family of stone carvers, told me that Spratling often brought designs to his father's workshop for objects he wanted made in stone.[34] Spratling is said to have had an "expert" in Taxco, a highly respected stone worker, who was often called out to the ranch to evaluate artifacts he himself had made. Was Spratling unknowingly buying this man's sculptures while at the same time hiring him to make others which he would sell to his North American friends as authentic? It was a tangled, nightmarish world.

Antonio Castillo has a small museum of pre-Columbian antiquities at his house and silver workshop at Taxco-el-viejo. When asked if Spratling bought many fakes, he said simply, "We all do."[35] The sellers come with boxes of pieces, most of it junk but with one or two fine pieces mixed in, and to get those, one has to buy the whole box.

Some of the faked pieces have gotten into the most prestigious museums, including the National Museum of Anthropology in Mexico City. A skilled stone artisan in Taxco is said to claim as his work several of the stone masks in the Mezcala style on exhibit in a room devoted to the art of West Mexico in the National Museum of Anthropology. The possible truth of that claim is corroborated by at least two experts who have said privately that three of the four large stone masks on a central panel in that room of the Museum are not authentic.

Spratling's friends are divided about the extent to which he knew that he was buying fakes in the last years of his life. One friend describes a trip to Iguala with Spratling during which one of Feliz Salgado de Gutiérrez's sons sold Spratling several very crude fake pieces. Finally unable to contain himself any longer, the friend pulled the young man aside and asked him how he could do such a thing to Don Guillermo. "Señor," the young man said with a gesture of despair. "What can I do? He isn't interested in the real pieces!"[36]

On the other hand, Spratling seemed to be deliberately building up a collection of fakes, which he kept in a special closet at the ranch. Did he regard it as a study collection, to teach himself the difference? Or did he use it to test his friends and other collectors? "What do you think?" he liked to say. Or "I'm 70 percent sure of it."[37]

In 1960 Spratling met Tatiana Proskouriakoff, a highly respected Maya scholar at the Peabody Museum at Harvard, and that fall he sent her a jade piece, asking her to evaluate it. When she questioned its attribution on several points, he responded that he shared her skepticism, but to a lesser degree, and so had decided to bet on authenticity.[38] That seemed in general to be his attitude. When he was not sure, he bet on authenticity and acted accordingly.

Proskouriakoff, for her part, recorded in her diary her attitude toward such consulting. "Spratling's sending me a jade! Will no one leave me alone! Most embarrassing to get mixed up with these collectors!"[39] Several months earlier, after meeting Spratling at a luncheon with several friends in Mexico City and then visiting Taxco to see his collections, she had written in her diary, "Beautiful pieces, but it is hard to tell the fakes from the true. The house is modest, old and charming—Spratling has true taste and it is a pity he isn't interested in history."[40]

Inevitably Spratling's dealing in dubious pieces strained his friendships. Rufino Tamayo bought an archaeological piece from Spratling that turned out to be fake. When he told Spratling this, the latter explained and apologized profusely and exchanged it for another. But the second one was also fake, and their friendship never recovered.[41] It was not an isolated instance.

Spratling liked to pretend that it did not matter whether a piece was authentic or a reproduction. What he was interested in, he insisted, was the skill of the artisan and the sculptural qualities of the piece itself. As Diego Rivera famously said, shrugging, on the question of fakes in his ceramic collection which he sometimes bought in bulk, without even bothering to open up the boxes, "Same clay. Same Indians."[42] If a pot is beautiful, does it matter whether it was made in A.D. 400 or 1960? But to an archaeologist or art scholar, it matters a great deal, for faked pieces undercut the very foundations of accurate data on which all their interpretations are based. And to a collector it matters, for no collector wants to pay for an authentic piece, only to have its value plummet when it is deemed a fake.

Spratling liked to play elaborate "cloak and dagger" games around the passing across the border of his artifacts. A jade mask wrapped in newspaper appeared in the middle of the night at the home of a curator at the Los Angeles County Museum. Spratling hoped that the curator might persuade the museum to buy it.[43] In another instance in 1959 Spratling telephoned his old friend René d'Harnoncourt, the director of the Museum of Modern Art in New York and an advisor to Nelson Rockefeller on acquisitions for a planned museum of primitive art, with an urgent message. He said he had something fabulous. He had gone into chicken farming and now owned seventeen golden chickens who behaved like young eagles. He wondered if their mutual friend up the river who owned a chicken farm might be interested in this new breed.[44] D'Harnoncourt interpreted the phone call, with the help of a photographic slide that arrived soon after, to mean that Spratling had a collection of pre-Columbian gold pieces that he wanted to sell to Nelson Rockefeller, at that time governor of New York (up the river at Albany). The collection included a spectacular necklace in the form of seventeen gold eagles, along with several other smaller items such as gold bells, a warrior figure, a bat, and an eagle head.

D'Harnoncourt was interested but wary. Rockefeller had made purchases before from Spratling, including a white Olmec head or mask for $4,000 and a Teotihuacan gray stone mask for $5,500 in 1957.[45] But this time the experts d'Harnoncourt consulted, including Gordon Eckholm, Samuel Lothrop, and Dudley Easby, were uncertain about the authenticity of the pieces.

Spratling, who had gone into debt to acquire the gold collection, waited impatiently in Taxco to learn whether Rockefeller was interested. Finally, after a couple of months, he sent d'Harnoncourt a telegram, again in code, hinting that his situation was grave and that he needed an immediate down payment on the possible purchase.[46] At d'Harnoncourt's urging, Rockefeller made a payment of $10,000, one-tenth of what Spratling was asking for the collection, and Spratling came himself to New York to pick up the check.[47]

When he got back to Taxco-el-viejo Spratling was jubilant. He called Carl Pappé in Taxco to say, "Carl, what's cooking? Can you lead me to anything? I just came back with a whole suitcase of money from selling to Rockefeller."[48]

But his joy was short-lived. Rockefeller finally bought only the necklace of gold eagles and for $25,000, which was half of what Spratling had hoped to get for it. Then the experts decided that it, too, was questionable. Spratling was obliged to

return the money or offer an equivalent in other pieces from his collection. Meanwhile collectors who had bought the smaller gold items began to want their money back. His financial situation, already precarious, became worse. The collecting of archaeological pieces which had brought him so much pleasure and sustained him financially through most of his years in Mexico was, in the end, his undoing.

In 1972, five years after Spratling's death, the Mexican government passed a new law which not only forbade exports but gave the state itself the sole right to buy or sell pre-Columbian artifacts. All Mexican collectors were required to register their collections with the government, after which time they could no longer buy or sell. The new law virtually put an end to private collecting in Mexico.

CHAPTER EIGHT

THE END OF THE ROAD

In his last years at the ranch Spratling followed a strict routine that seemed designed to give meaning, or at least order, to his life. He rose at 5:30 A.M. and worked in the morning. Lunch at 12:30 was prepared by Antonio, the cook, and was preceded by martinis mixed with great ceremony according to Spratling's special formula. Frequently there were guests, and the food was superb, perhaps a fresh river Guerrero fish with Hollandaise sauce, Bibb lettuce from Spratling's garden, and popovers, which were Antonio's specialty. The room was simple, the wood furniture rough. "His decor was nothing," one friend remembers, "not even an upholstered sofa. You sat on wooden chairs."[1] But the napkins would be perfectly starched and Spratling managed to convey a sense of elegance that reminded at least some of his visitors of midtown New York.

After lunch Spratling took a nap. At 3:00 P.M. he greeted tourists who were brought by taxi drivers or guides. Many Taxco taxis had a sign, "Visite Spratling" in their rear windows. For a set fee, the driver would take tourists to the Spratling ranch and receive in return a commission on all purchases.[2] Spratling evaluated his customers and offered them silver, gold, or archaeological pieces according to what he thought they could afford. A gold room had on exhibit his most special pieces, and there he served iced champagne. Another room had a display of silver, and there he served tequila. Then there was the shop, open to tourists in general.[3]

At night after the workshop was closed and the last of his clients had gone, Spratling drank whisky sours made with two kinds of oranges cultivated on his ranch. In good company, after three or four drinks he would begin telling stories—about Faulkner tearing up an unpublished novel and throwing it overboard as they crossed the Atlantic, about the campesinos who came at night to sell him artifacts they had dug up in the fields, about his little airplane hitting a mountaintop in the fog when he was on his way to Mexico City to meet John Huston.[4] If on other nights he was bored with his guests, he might simply let the generator go off at 8:30 as it did routinely, and go to bed, leaving them in the dark.

Once a week, on Mondays, Spratling drove with a chauffeur to Mexico City. 113

William Spratling. Photo
courtesy of Alfonso Soto Soria.

These weekly trips were a routine in themselves. Spratling left at 5:30 A.M. and
breakfasted with friends in Mexico City, usually with the sculptor Helen Escobedo, who had worked with him on two exhibits at the Museum at the National
University of Mexico. Then he delivered silver orders and made the rounds of
galleries and shops that sold silver and pre-Columbian art, buying, selling, and

bartering as he went. He went to the Turkish baths, met friends for lunch at his favorite restaurant, the Bellinghausen, and at 3 P.M. left for home, stopping at a supermarket on the way out of town. He drove to Mexico City but let his chauffeur drive on their return, and they had an on-going contest to see who could make the roughly three-hour trip in the least time.

With good friends, Spratling was very open about his activities at the baths in Mexico City, his attitude being that they ought to try it, that it was just another activity he pioneered, that he enjoyed it enormously and they would too if they would lose their inhibitions.

Spratling's house at the ranch was a simple structure, crammed full of paintings by Diego Rivera, Siqueiros, and others, piled with pre-Columbian stone and clay pieces and pottery and with masks looking down from the walls. One friend called it "a kind of haphazard masterpiece" with idols spilling out of the house into the overgrown gardens. At night one could hear the sounds of the river flowing along his "wild, fertile property."[5] It was enchanting but intimidating for it was awesome and semiwild, like Spratling himself.

For Spratling had become a rather difficult character. His moods were nothing new. Even Covarrubias, years before, while urging a friend who was going to Taxco to look up Spratling, had warned, "You will find him the most charming man you ever met—unless he has had a bad day. Then he may be the most difficult S.O.B. you ever met."[6] The intervening years of loneliness, of financial difficulties, of recurring legal problems surrounding his collecting activities, and of drinking had not improved his temperament. He had been surpassed in the silver business by his former apprentices. He had been outdone in archaeological collecting by newcomers who had far greater resources than he had. His old friend William Faulkner had won a Nobel Prize for Literature in 1949, but he was having to beg a publisher to do a new edition of his long-out-of-print *Little Mexico*. Little wonder that he was touchy, that he was sometimes bitter, and that he seemed to take perverse delight in unsettling others by frightening or embarrassing them. His "jokes" ranged from pretending in mid-flight that his plane was about to lose a wing to serving ice cream in which a chunk of quartz was imbedded.

Spratling dealt with his loneliness by telephoning friends all over Mexico and around the world, and by surrounding himself with animals. He raised Great Dane dogs and sometimes had as many as twenty-three of them. When they misbehaved, he shot a water pistol at them. He had Siamese cats and later Abyssinian cats, an ocelot, a pair of otters, and a parrot. He taught the parrot to ring a large bronze bell brought from the La Florida workshop by pulling on a wire. He had it rung every day at 8 A.M., 1 P.M., 2 P.M., and 5 P.M. to signal the opening and closing of the silver workshop.[7]

One Cuernavaca friend, Deva Garro, thought that Spratling's life at the ranch was sad, for Taxco-el-viejo was "a dusty little town," and he was very isolated there. When she and her artist husband visited Spratling, he would proudly show them the small museum he had built to house his archaeological collection, but it seemed to her dark and dusty. He no longer was much interested in designing new silver pieces.[8]

Part of Spratling's isolation came, ironically, from the respect, even reverence, his former apprentices still felt for him. "Call me Bill," he would urge them, and they would reply, "Don Guillermo, I just can't. You were my maestro, my teacher."[9]

"I called him Bill," Antonio Pineda told me proudly. "I was the only one that did."[10] But Pineda worked for Spratling only briefly, twice, during summer vacations, and as one of the leading silversmiths (and prize-winners) of Taxco has been particularly eager to emphasize his independence from the Spratling tradition.

In 1962 Antonio Castillo bought land at Taxco-el-viejo just two kilometers up the road from Spratling's and began to build a house there. When Spratling learned about Castillo's plans, he urged him to build farther back on the property, across the river and away from the noise of the road, and he offered his services as an architect to make the drawings for the house as a gift to Castillo. But the latter gently refused. "He was a very strong character, you know," Castillo said years later.

> I said to myself, he is one of my best friends and I have great respect for him as my patron . . . , my teacher. But I wanted to have my house where I wanted it and I wanted it to be my house, not to be Spratling's house. . . . But it hurt him very much that I did not accept his proposition. For three months he did not speak to me, and for one year he did not visit me at my house.[11]

Antonio Castillo is such a gentle, loving man that no one, not even Bill Spratling, could stay angry with him for long. They resumed their thirty-year-old and close friendship but always with the traditional pattern of deference. Castillo would consider any request from Spratling, even an impromptu invitation to come over for coffee, as having priority over whatever else he was doing, and he always called him Don Guillermo.

In his last years Spratling did take special pride in the little museum he built at the ranch. The impetus was a theft, which he felt must be an inside job. So he converted an old outdoor pillared walkway into an L-shaped museum that had only one door. He kept it locked, and he had the only key. The museum was a very simple but ingeniously designed structure, with fifty-eight niches in the walls

Spratling's museum, from *William* Spratling by Ruby N. Castrejón and Jaime Castrejón D. (n.p., n.d., c. 1968), pamphlet published as a fundraiser for the Museum of Taxco.

which were covered with plastic, so that the room was lit entirely by natural daylight. The niches were painted different bright colors such as yellow and red. In these he arranged his archaeological collection: stone sculptures of men, animals, and temples from Guerrero, a Nayarit clay figure of a woman, "laughing" Remojadas figures, carvings in alabaster and jade, a rare funerary offering from Teotihuacan, a large stone egg. In 1965 the *Architectural Digest* ran a six page spread of photographs of the museum and the William Spratling collection it housed. He sent a reprint to Tatiana Proskouriakoff, with his card and a note inviting her to come down and see it.[12]

Spratling had always had a talent for publicity. He liked to read his name in the newspaper, and he liked to entertain prestigious visitors and celebrities at the ranch. He was proud of having been visited there by both Richard and Pat Nixon and by Lyndon and Lady Bird Johnson. Film director John Huston was a frequent visitor and a frequent buyer of silver and pre-Columbian art.

Stanley Marcus, the Texas retailer, remembers the ranch as "a nice place to visit." Spratling was "very *simpatico,*" Marcus recalls, but not a good businessman. "Bill was always broke—always in need of money." One night at Paco's Bar after the third tequila, Spratling confessed that a creditor was pressing him. "I'll sell you the painting you like [a nineteenth-century oil of the cathedral square in Puebla] and the Archipenko sculpture," he offered. So Marcus bought them. Marcus also bought many pieces of Spratling silver on his own account and tried to carry Spratling silver in his store, but Spratling would not give him a wholesale price. In one Marcus-related incident which Spratling liked to recount, he was delivering silver and a present of strawberries from his garden to Stanley Marcus in Mexico City via his airplane, when shortly after take-off the plane fell back to earth and turned over in a mud bank. Spratling arrived two hours late at their place of meeting, and he and his packages appeared to be covered with blood, but it was only strawberry juice.[13]

Marilyn Monroe made a visit to the ranch in February of 1962. She had recently bought a Spanish-style house in Brentwood and was shopping for furnishings in Mexico. Frederick and Nieves Field took her to Taxco where she bought wood and leather furniture and glass and metal lighting fixtures at the Taller Borda, and they all spent the night in a small hotel, a former convent, called Los Arcos. The next day they were invited to the Spratling ranch for lunch. The actress admired Spratling's round dining table of native mahogany on a scalloped octagonal base and ordered one just like it for herself. Marilyn Monroe's companion, Eunice Murray, remembered Spratling as a tall, graying man in his sixties who showed them around his workshops, accompanied wherever he went by his troop of large Great Danes. It was Marilyn Monroe's last real holiday. Six months later she was dead.[14]

In 1964 Spratling had a serious airplane accident. En route to Mexico City early one morning where he was to deliver some silver to John Huston and have breakfast with him, he lost control of his plane in a sudden storm and ran into a mountain. He had the presence of mind to cut off the gas and turn off the engine just before he hit, so the plane did not catch fire, but it was crushed, rammed nose-first into the ground at a 30 degree angle. Spratling hopped out, realizing that it was a miracle that he was still alive. But the plane was destroyed. He found himself trapped in a thick fog on a mountaintop, at an altitude of 11,800 feet, with no alternative but to crawl back into the wrecked plane, for he did not know where he was. He spent all day there without food or water. At dusk he wrote a brief will and signed it, scarcely expecting to survive the bitter cold of the coming night. But he did. The next morning the clouds lifted, and he could see a small village about twenty miles away. He walked to it, accompanied for the last half of the way by an old Indian he met along the way who sewed up his torn shoes with a thread of maguey fiber. In the village he got a truck driver to take him to Xochimilco and from there he took a cab to Mexico City.

A helicopter pilot sent to look for another, large plane eventually found Sprat-

ling's Ercoupe and salvaged the aluminum propeller.[15] Spratling kept the propeller thereafter in a corner of his living room, a monument to the plane that had
provided him with so much pleasure for sixteen years, but perhaps also a *memento*
mori in the Mexican sense, an ever-present reminder of death that now seemed to
haunt him. It was after the accident that he left a sealed envelope with his secretary. On the outside he wrote, "Closed until you have notice of my not coming
back." Inside were instructions on how his business should be turned into a cooperative run by the workers.[16]

The accident scared him enough so that he turned in his license and swore off
flying. But he yearned to fly again and kept threatening to buy another airplane, "if
he could find one he liked." He told his secretary, as if he were telling himself, how
much more probable it was that he would die in a car accident than in a plane.

Sometimes he was willing, if a journalist caught him in the right mood, to
reflect on his life in Mexico and on the differences between Mexicans and Americans. Mexicans find American tourists shocking, he told one such visitor, because
of their voices. "Americans raise their voices. In Mexico it is an insult to raise one's
voice, even in anger, and the natives . . . never get over being shocked at American
tourists shouting to each other across the plaza."

He didn't consider himself Mexican. "No, I'm just a Mexicanized gringo. But
that is better than being a gringoized Mexican, such as flourish in Mexico City."
By and large he thought Mexicans are "more tolerant and less censorious of others
than we are. The innate courtesy that you find in even the most uneducated
Indian does not exist in the United States."[17]

A new edition of *Little Mexico* appeared in 1964, published by Little, Brown
and Company, with an introductory note by John Huston. Spratling added a new
foreword, quoting a provincial verse to express his feeling for what had become his
own *patria chica* (homeland):

Cuando yo muera, comadre,
Haga de mi barro un jarro,
Si tienes sed, de mi bebe,
Y si a tus labios el barro se pega,
Es un beso de tu charro.
When I die, my dear,
Of my clay make a cup,
When you have thirst, from me drink,
The clay which clings to your lips
Is a kiss from your lover.

The new edition of *Little Mexico* was celebrated with a reception in Mexico City on February 13, 1965, the first of several instances of welcome publicity for Spratling that year. He was honored at the reception for his work in improving cultural relations between Mexico and the United States, and a booklet was published to record the proceedings. The film short about Spratling, "The Man from New Orleans" was shown, and John L. Brown, the cultural attaché at the United States Embassy in Mexico, spoke, as did Luis Avéleyra Arroyo de Anda, secretary general of the National Museum of Anthropology. Aveleyra praised Spratling for his "solid and profound knowledge" of Mexico, "based on daily contact, year after year, with our rural people," and of his opening up to the world with Covarrubias the extraordinary Mezcala style. Spratling's appreciation for the true value of Mexico is "perhaps more than any other person of foreign origin has been able to achieve," Aveleyra said. Mexican historian Rafael S. Muñoz spoke of Spratling's having given "a spirit of creation" to the town of Taxco before known only for its church and its narrow streets.[18] Spratling was visibly moved by the testimonies. What Helen Escobedo remembers most about the occasion was how lonely he seemed. She and her husband had been invited to join Spratling in his hotel room for a private party before the reception. They went expecting to find a large crowd present, but there were only one or two other guests.

Another welcome tribute was an exhibit called "The World of William Spratling," put together by John Leeper at the McNay Museum in San Antonio, Texas. The exhibit included not only Spratling silver and works in gold but also pre-Columbian, African, and Oceanic sculpture from his collection, manuscripts and illustrations from his publications, his drawings and lithographs, and letters and autographs from Rivera and Covarrubias. In the commentary Leeper tried to animate these object by giving the feel of a visit to Spratling's ranch—the low house surrounded by Aztec sculptures and overgrown plants with bougainvillea climbing up the walls, the dusty interior with masks from Alaska, a jade spoon from China, piles of books with letters and sketches falling out of them.[19] The exhibit traveled to eleven cities in the United States, all of them initiated by Spratling himself except the originating McNay Museum, and Spratling went to the opening at the Otis Art Institute in Los Angeles. He obviously liked the title of the exhibit for he dedicated his autobiography *File on Spratling* "To James Thurber, also a draftsman, who wrote *My World, and Welcome to It* [,] alas, what a title!" But the world the exhibit portrayed was that of Spratling's last years at the ranch. It was not the world of William Spratling of the late 1930s when he had been at the peak of his success, striding through the town of Taxco as its *patrón,* as the rock on which their economic miracle was built, surrounded by a community that was like an extended family, and he was at the center of it, the father figure, greeting

Spratling at the Los Angeles
opening of "The World of
William Spratling," 1965.
Photo courtesy of Stanley
Marcus.

everyone by name. "The World of William Spratling" is a world with only one
person—himself—in it, apart from the famous friends whose mention there is less
a tribute to their friendship than an attempt to bolster Spratling's importance.

Taxco's annual Silver Fair, which had begun as a celebration of the founding of
Spratling's workshop, had grown into an event that was an official state holiday.
Spratling had stayed away from it for years, but in 1965 Ted Wick, a Hollywood

publicist who had just moved to Taxco, arranged to have Gloria Swanson come as a special guest. Who should escort her, he asked Spratling, the municipal president or the governor of the state of Guerrero? Who was the better dancer? Wick's ruse worked. Spratling decided that he could dust off his old tuxedo and escort Gloria Swanson, and so he did.[20]

Spratling liked the idea of writing his memoirs, but when it came time to do it, he was stymied. He hated having to be less than honest, and yet he knew there were aspects of his life the public would find scandalous. But Little, Brown and Company had published a new edition of *Little Mexico* with the expectation that his memoirs would be forthcoming, and they sent literary agent and editor Gerald R. Kelly to Taxco-el-viejo in the summer of 1966 with a tape recorder. Spratling and Kelly had many taping sessions, usually in the evening over drinks, but whenever they came to anything sensitive Spratling would turn off the tape recorder and then go on talking. "He was really very rigid about what he wanted in and what he wanted out of the book, which was really too bad because he was a much more fascinating character than the book shows," Kelly said years later.[21] Spratling reminisced and, with some prodding, told anecdotes about famous people he had known. He defended his collecting and trading activities and made careful drawings of the layout of his house in Taxco and of his ranch. With these materials and large chunks from Spratling's previous writings, Kelly managed to put the book together. The cover is splendid—a reproduction of Siqueiros's oil portrait of the subject—but the contents less satisfying. One critic deplored the "sad posturing" in the book, especially when compared to the freshness of the author's *Little Mexico,* written thirty-five years before.[22] And some of Spratling's friends felt they could scarcely recognize the modest, self-effacing man they knew in the crude anecdote-telling man the book portrayed.

In his last years Spratling corresponded occasionally with the artist-turned-archaeologist Tatiana Proskouriakoff, whose unquestioned intelligence and integrity, like Elizabeth Anderson's, attracted him. Both women were, in effect, moral lodestones for him. If they understood him, and approved of him, he did not much care what the rest of the world thought, or so he tried to convince himself. Late in 1966 he wrote Proskouriakoff, urging her not to believe the things she had said she was hearing about him. If it was his collecting activities, he had little to conceal or apologize for, he assured her. And if it was his private life, well, that was his own business. Might we not all appear monsters if our innermost secrets were revealed, he wondered.[23]

Spratling had a prostate operation in May of 1967. After that, according to his long-time secretary Margarita González Banda, he seemed to grow old, to feel old. He went much less often to the workshop and the salesroom. He spent his time drinking and sleeping. Often he would begin drinking at 8 A.M., which he had never done before. The employees always called him "Don Guillermo," but behind his back now he was "el viejo" [the old man].

The question of what to do with his archaeology collection bothered Spratling increasingly, as he seemed to feel that his end was near. He had made large gifts to the Museum of the National University of Mexico and to the new Anthropology Museum,[24] but still there was his private collection. He began to have long conversations about it with Jaime Castrejón, the young reformist municipal president of Taxco.

On Sunday, August 6, 1967, a couple from the United States wanted to see his museum. He never opened it on Sunday, but that day he did, saying, "Probably I will die tomorrow and next year when you come there won't be any Spratling gallery."[25]

Earlier that day he had gone to brunch at Ted Wick's. Ted Wick had built himself a large house next to the El Solar mine on a hill overlooking Taxco. Spratling and Elizabeth Anderson and Wick stood on the terrace that morning and looked down at the cemetery which lay at the bottom of the hill in front of the house, laughing about the special "Gringo Section" that had been purchased and fenced off by a group of thirteen expatriates from the United Stated who wanted to make sure their graves would not be trampled on. They had already cemented the vaults so that all that remained to be done was drop in the coffins and cement them in. "Can you imagine being buried with those people!" Spratling snorted with disgust. He intended to be cremated, he told them, and did not want any fuss about a funeral.[26]

That night about ten o'clock he telephoned Ruby Castrejón, wanting to make certain that the plans he had made for transforming his personal collection into a museum for the city of Taxco were all in order.[27]

Early Monday morning, August 7, 1967, he set out at 5 A.M. in his new Mustang for his weekly trip to Mexico City with his chauffeur. The highway was still wet from a storm the night before, but he drove at breakneck speed as always. South of Iguala at Tinajillas he swerved to avoid a tree that had fallen across the road during the night and crashed the car into another tree. He was thrown against the steering wheel and some ribs were smashed. But he was still conscious.

The chauffeur was shaken up but unhurt and ran down the road to call an ambulance, which arrived about forty minutes after the accident. Spratling was taken to a doctor's office in Iguala, where he was X-rayed. He asked for a cup of coffee and talked to Antonio, his houseman and chef. "*A ver si esta vez no me muero,*" he said. (Let's see if I survive this one.)[28] A short time later he died, of a heart attack, in the ambulance that was taking him to the hospital.

"*A ver que sale,*" Mexicans say. "Let's see what comes of it." By the end of his life Spratling had absorbed this attitude which connotes, not fatalism, but the more activist psychology of the gambler. Let's throw the dice and see what comes of it.[29] And that is the way he chose to live his life.

Tasqueños remember August 7, 1967, the day Spratling died, as North Americans of at least a certain age remember the deaths of John F. Kennedy and Franklin D. Roosevelt—they can remember what they were doing when they heard the news. "I was in Mexico City when I got a phone call, and immediately I came back to Taxco," they say, or "I heard it when I walked down to the *zócalo.*" Elizabeth Anderson learned about it at mid-morning and stumbled out of the door to take a taxi to Spratling's ranch. Already black bows were being placed across shop windows. The taxi driver gave her a sad nod of the head, and they drove in silence the ten miles to Taxco-el-viejo. The house was already surrounded by police, who were sealing it.

It was soon evident a quiet cremation was impossible, given the unexpected outpouring of emotion and the calls for public homage. Spratling's body was brought in a procession back to Taxco, the town he had scarcely set foot in for more than ten years, for even on his weekly trips to Mexico City, he scrupulously avoided the road that went through Taxco and took the Iguala route instead. His expensive gray coffin was carried to the ceremonial room on the top floor of the City Hall, and there his body lay in state as hundreds of people passed by to say farewell. Old women following local custom, leaned over to grasp his feet, murmuring, "Adiós, may you go well, and may these feet carry you to heaven."[30] At six P.M. the casket was closed, and his friends and former employees took turns standing vigil throughout the night.

An immediate problem was where his body should be buried. Then it was learned that one of the thirteen Americans who had prepared a grave site in the "Gringo Section" of the cemetery had since left Taxco, and that grave was bought for Spratling.[31] He would be buried in the place he had scorned just three days earlier.

Twenty thousand people went to the funeral the next afternoon. That at least was the number estimated by a reporter for the English language newspaper, *The News,* published in Mexico City.[32] Shops in Taxco were closed and the windows hung with black bows. The church of Santa Prisca filled with people and the overflow spilled out into the atrium, down the steps, and into the square until it

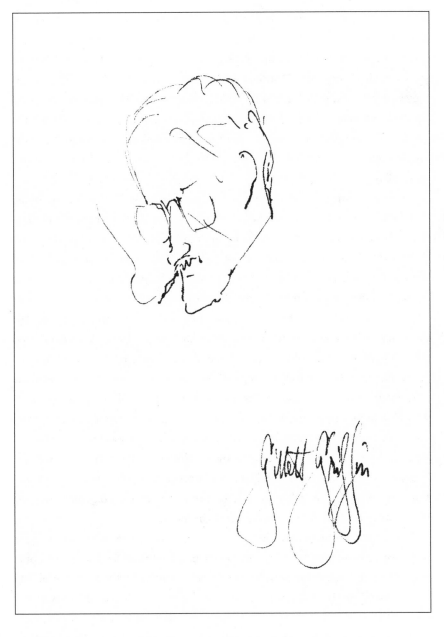

Gillett Griffin, sketch of
William Spratling. Collection
of the author.

too was jam-packed. People climbed on rooftops and crowded together at upper-story windows. An enormous bank of flowers extended for a hundred feet along the side of the church. Elizabeth Anderson was astonished at the crowd and surprised particularly by the number of little old Taxco ladies dressed in black who attended the funeral.[33] He was more loved than he knew, she wrote Caroline Durieux. She herself missed Bill terribly.[34]

Shortly before four o'clock a procession led by John L. Brown, the cultural attaché from the United States Embassy in Mexico City, Jaime Castrejón, the municipal president of Taxco, Antonio Castillo, Margarita Domínguez Islas, and several other old friends of Spratling's moved from the City Hall up the steep streets to the Santa Prisca church. Ten silversmiths, all Spratling's former employees, carried the casket into the church for the mass which was broadcast over a squawking loudspeaker to the crowd in the plaza. Then the procession left the church and moved on foot, as was traditional, through the town and down the long descending road to the cemetery, with people following on foot and in cars and trucks.

At the graveside John Brown and Jaime Castrejón spoke briefly, but the tribute that people remember was by Margarita Domínguez Islas. A woman in her late sixties, from an old Taxco family (her grandmother had sold Spratling his house on the Calle de las Delicias), she had been a schoolteacher until around 1939 when she was put in charge of the government office which Spratling helped set up that guaranteed the silver content of the pieces produced in the town. "The people of Taxco are in mourning," she began. Then she spoke, for almost half an hour, of the man who had come to settle among them "not just as a friend, but as a brother, who for more than thirty-five years had shared our pains, our bitter griefs, our sorrows, and our poverty as well as our pleasures and deepest joys." She reminded the crowd that when Spratling settled in Taxco the town was still struggling with the wounds and bitter legacies of the revolution and needed to rebuild itself up from economic ruin so that its people could start a new life. "It was Don Guillermo," she said, "who was the basic pillar of the new industry,"[35] the silver industry which had brought prosperity and world fame to the town. Margarita Domínguez knew, from the amount of silver that she processed and stamped every day, just how great the prosperity was that Spratling had brought them.

Margarita Domínguez was herself a pillar in Taxco, one of the town's most respected citizens. Twenty-five years later when I went to see her in her home behind one of the shops on Merchants Street, she was too ill that Sunday morning to keep our appointment, but her brother and sister filled in for her. They served me a special nut liquor, an *infusión de nogal* and talked about the past.

"Why are there so few traces of Spratling in the town today?" I wondered.

They shook their heads. "Taxco has changed so much. So many new people have come to town," they said, sighing. "But the true Tasqueños appreciate him."[36]

NOTES

INTRODUCTION

1. William P. Spratling, "Some Impressions of Mexico," Part 1, *The Architectural Forum* 47, no. 1 (July 1927): 1. Also William Spratling, "Guanajuato, the Most Mexican City," Part 1, *The Architectural Forum* (February 1928): 217–18, and William Spratling, "Mexican Letter," *New York Herald Tribune,* Books (March 24, 1929): xi.
2. William Spratling, "The Silver City of the Clouds," *Travel* 53, no. 3 (July 1929): 22–23.
   A good short history of Taxco is Jaime Castrejón Díez, "Taxco and Its Origins," *Artes de Mexico* 5 (Fall 1989): 82–85.

CHAPTER ONE

1. Smith Ely Jelliffe, "Obituaries: William P. Spratling," *The Journal of Nervous and Mental Diseases* 45 (1917): 191–92.
2. William Spratling, *File on Spratling* (Boston: Little, Brown, 1967), 7.
3. Ed [Bleier] to Bill, n.d., but c. January 1947, Spratling Ranch Archives.
4. Natalie Scott, clippings from "Peggy Passe Partout, *New Orleans States,* n.d., Natalie Scott Papers, Special Collections, Tulane University Library.
5. Oliver La Farge, *Raw Material* (Boston: Houghton Mifflin, 1945), 127.
6. Clippings, William Spratling file, New Orleans Historical Collection.
7. James G. Watson, ed., *Thinking of Home: William Faulkner's Letters to His Mother and Father, 1918–1925* (New York: Norton, 1992), 187.
8. Frederick R. Karl, *William Faulkner: American Writer* (New York: Ballantine Books, 1989), 202.
9. Spratling, *File on Spratling,* 30.
10. William Faulkner, *Mosquitoes* (New York: Liveright, 1955 [orig. 1927]), p. 231. Spratling tells the same story in *File on Spratling,* 15.

11. William Faulkner, *New Orleans Sketches,* edited by Carvel Collins (New York: Random House, 1968), 46–54. In another sketch, "Episode," Spratling calls down from his balcony to an elderly couple, and they pose for him as Faulkner ruminates on what they are thinking.

12. William P. Spratling, *Pencil Drawing,* n.p.

13. Anon., *New Orleans States* (October 19, 1927) clipping in William Spratling file, New Orleans Historical Collection.

14. Vera Morel, "Skills of Local Artists Attract Many," n.d., n.p., clipping in William Spratling file, New Orleans Historical Collection.

15. Meigs O. Frost, "Splendid Exhibit at Orleans Arts and Crafts," *New Orleans States* (November 26, 1925), clipping in William Spratling file, New Orleans Historical Collection.

16. Interview with Enrique Alferez, January 21, 1998.

17. Natalie Scott, clippings from "Peggy Passe Partout."

18. *Southern Odyssey: Selected Writings by Sherwood Anderson,* edited by Welford Dunaway Taylor and Charles E. Modlin (Athens: University of Georgia Press, 1997), 44.

19. Joseph Blotner, *Faulkner: A Biography,* 2 vols. (New York: Random House, 1974), 585. Also Lyle Saxon to anon., January 13, 1929, Lyle Saxon Papers, Special Collections, Tulane University Library.

20. Joe to Lyle Saxon, February 13, 1929, Lyle Saxon Papers.

21. Leslie C. De Figueroa, *Stuffed Shirt in Taxco* (Taxco: Taxco School of Art, 1961), 132, on nervous breakdown. Dolores Olmedo in William Spratling, *México tras lomita,* with Prólogo by José N. Iturriaga (Mexico: Editorial Diana, 1991), 41; also interview with Olmedo, January 1995.

22. William Spratling, review of *Marie Bonifas* by Jacques de Lauretelle, *New York Herald Tribune,* Section 11, Books (Sunday, June 2, 1929): 16. See Bibliography for a full list of Spratling's contributions to the Books Section of the *New York Herald Tribune.*

CHAPTER TWO

1. "Spratling descubre un importante códice," clipping, dated August 29, 1929, Special Collections, Tulane University Library.

2. Elizabeth Morrow, *The Mexican Years* (New York: Spiral Press, 1953), 256.

3. Spratling, *File on Spratling,* 108.

4. Spratling to Carl Zigrosser, October 19, 1931, Carl Zigrosser Papers, Archives of American Art, Smithsonian Institution. Spratling, "Literary Notes from Mexico," in *New York Herald Tribune,* Books (March 8, 1931).

5. Raquel Tibol, "David Alfaro Siqueiros in Taxco," in *Artes de México* 5 (Fall 1989): 94, 95.

6. Spratling to Carl Zigrosser, December 26, 1931; also October 19, 1931, Carl Zigrosser Papers.

7. Spratling, "The Arts and Letters in Mexico," Books, *New York Herald Tribune* (June 8, 1930): 9.

8. Spratling, *México tras lomita,* Prólogo de José N. Iturriaga (Mexico: Editorial Diana), 61.

9. Interview with Enrique Alferez, January 21, 1998.

10. Spratling, *File on Spratling,* 153.

11. *Mexican Folkways* 6, nos. 1 and 2 (1930).

12. Carleton Beals, *The Great Circle: Further Adventures in Free-Lancing* (Philadelphia: J. B. Lippincott, 1940), 328–29.

13. Spratling, *File on Spratling,* 41–42.

14. Stuart Chase, *Mexico, A Study of Two Americas* (New York: Macmillan, 1931), 23.

15. Helen Delpar, *The Enormous Vogue of Things Mexican: Cultural Relations Between the United States and Mexico, 1920–1935* (Tuscaloosa: University of Alabama Press, 1992), 100.

16. Ibid., 123.

17. Stuart Chase, review of Spratling, *Little Mexico,* in *New York Herald Tribune, Books* (February 24, 1932): 5.

18. Quoted in Kim Townsend, *Sherwood Anderson* (Boston: Houghton Mifflin, 1987), 250.

19. Interview with Gobi Stromberg, January 1993. For Anderson on Spratling, see Elizabeth Anderson, and Gerald R. Kelly, *Miss Elizabeth: A Memoir* (Boston: Little, Brown, 1969), 206.

20. Peter T. Furst, Foreword to Donald Cordry, *Mexican Masks* (Austin: University of Texas Press, 1980), x.

21. Spratling to Carl Zigrosser, November 22, 1931, Carl Zigrosser Papers, Archives of American Art, Smithsonian Institution.

22. Interview with Antonio Castillo, January 1993.

23. Spratling, *File on Spratling,* 99.

24. Hart Crane to Samuel Loverman, November 17, 1931, in Brom Weber, ed., *The Letters of Hart Crane, 1916–1932* (New York: Hermitage House, 1952), 388.

25. Hart Crane to Malcolm Cowley, June 2, 1931, in Susan Jenkins Brown, *Robber Rocks: Letters and Memories of Hart Crane, 1923–1932* (Middletown, Conn.: Wesleyan University Press, 1969), 124–25.

26. Spratling to Zigrosser, June 8, 1930. Carl Zigrosser Papers, Archives of American Art, Smithsonian Institution.

27. Spratling to Zigrosser, June 4, 1932. Carl Zigrosser Papers, Archives of American Art, Smithsonian Institution.

28. Hart Crane to Solomon Grunberg, March 20, 1932, in Weber, *The Letters of Hart Crane,* 303.

29. Hart Crane to Malcolm Cowley, January 9, 1932, in Weber, *The Letters of Hart Crane,* 394.

30. Quoted in Helen Delpar, *The Enormous Vogue of Things Mexican,* 67.

31. Aldous Huxley, *Beyond the Mexique Bay,* 287.

32. Anderson and Kelly, *Miss Elizabeth: A Memoir,* 223–24.

CHAPTER THREE

1. Spratling to Zigrosser, March 4, 1932, Carl Zigrosser Papers, Archives of American Art, Smithsonian Institution.

2. Frederick Karl, *William Faulkner,* 223.

3. Carvel Collins, ed., *William Faulkner: New Orleans Sketches* (New York: Random House, 1958), xxviii.

4. William Spratling, *Escultura precolumbina de Guerrero* (Mexico: UNAM, 1964).

5. William Spratling, *A Small Mexican World* (Boston: Little, Brown, 1964). All quotations in this chapter are from this book unless otherwise noted.

6. Janet Mandelstam, "every taxco cloud has a silver lining," *The News* (Mexico City, February 12, 1965), clipping at the Spratling ranch.

7. Quoted in W. Kenneth Holditch, "William Faulkner, William Spratling, and Other Famous Creoles," unpublished ms.

8. C. G. Poore, "A Corner of the Mexican Maze," in *New York Times,* Books (July 31, 1932): 3.

9. Letter from William Spratling, *New York Times,* Books (September 25, 1932): 20.

10. Interview with Ted Wick, January 17, 1992.

11. Stuart Chase, review of *Little Mexico,* in *New York Herald Tribune* (February 14, 1932): 5.

12. John Chamberlain, "Books of the Times," *New York Times* (August 15, 1934): 15.

13. Stuart Chase, *Mexico: A Study of Two Americas,* 9, 17.

14. Haniel Long to Spratling, 1935, Spratling Ranch Archives.

CHAPTER FOUR

1. Spratling to Zigrosser, January 10, 1933, Carl Zigrosser Papers, Archives of American Art, Smithsonian Institution.

2. Mary L. Davis and Greta Pack, *Mexican Jewelry* (Austin: University of Texas Press, 1963), 160, 165.

3. Spratling, "Modern Mexican Silvermaking," *Mexican Art and Life* 3 (1937): 34.

4. Lucia Garcia Noriega Nieto, "Mexican Silver: William Spratling and the Taxco Style," trans. by Ahmed Simeon, *Journal of Decorative and Propaganda Arts* (Fall 1988): 43–53, 44.

5. Interview with Antonio Castillo, January 26, 1993.

6. Spratling, *File on Spratling.* 70.

7. Spratling, "25 Years of Mexican Silverware," *Artes de México* 3, no. 10 (1955): 87–90, 88.

8. Penny Chittim Morrill and Carole A. Berk, *Mexican Silver* (Atglen, Penn., Schiffer Publishing Co., 1994), 32–33.

9. Vladimiro Rosado Ojeda, "El oro y la plata en el México antiguo,*" Artes de Mexico* 3, no. 10(1955): 5–19, 7; Frances F. Berdan, "The Economics of Aztec Luxury Trade and Tribute," in Elizabeth Hill Boone, ed. *The Aztec Templo Mayor* (Washington, D.C.: Dumbarton Oaks, 1987), 161–83, 167.

10. Spratling, *File on Spratling,* 72.

11. Ibid., 83.

12. Ibid., 82; clipping, Mexican paper, n.d., Spratling Ranch Archives.

13. Margarita Domínguez Islas, *Taxco histórico, biográfico, anecdótico y legendario* (Acapulco, 1980), 135–36.

14. Iturriaga, ed., Prólogo to William Spratling, *México tras lomita* (Mexico: Editorial Diana, 1991), 52, quoting A. Castillo [author's translation].

15. Davis and Pack, *Mexican Jewelry,* 179.

16. Daniel F. Rubin de la Borbolla, "William Spratling, Pionero," pamphlet, n.p., accompanying *William Spratling Design Portfolio,* published by the Centro Cultural Arte Contemporáneo, Mexico City, 1987.

17. Interview with Antonio Castillo, January 26, 1993.

18. Interview with Teresa Domínguez Islas and Efrim Domínguez, January 31, 1993.

19. Interview with Carl Pappé, January 27, 1993.

20. Spratling, *File on Spratling,* 65.

21. Gobi Stromberg, *El juego del coyote: Platería y arte en Taxco* (Mexico: Fonda de Cultura Económica, 1985).

22. Spratling, *File on Spratling*, 3.

23. Ibid., 5.

24. William Spratling, "Un viajero alucinado en México" *Excelsio*r (September 27, 1928) clipping in Spratling Ranch Archives, Sucs. de William Spratling, S.A., Taxco-el-viejo, courtesy of Alberto Ulrich.

25. William Spratling, "Twenty-five years of Mexican Silverware," *Artes de Mexico* 10 (December 1955): 87–90, 87.

26. Spratling, *File on Spratling*, 83.

27. William Spratling, "Platería mexicana moderna," from *Mexican Life*, 1939, reprinted in *William Spratling Silver*, exhibit catalogue (Mexico: Centro Cultural/Arte Contemporáneo, 1987), 35.

28. Iturriaga, Prólogo to William Spratling, *México tras lomita*, interview with Tomás Vega, 59, translated by author.

29. Holland McCombs, "Articrafter of Taxco," ms, 5, 1942, Holland McCombs Papers, Special Collections, Paul Meek Library, University of Tennessee.

30. Interview with Carl Pappé, January 27, 1993.

31. Interview with Margarita González Banda, January 21, 1992.

32. Interview with Antonio Castillo, January 1993.

33. Interview by telephone with Stanley Marcus, June 28, 1995.

34. Margarita Domínguez Islas, *Taxco histórica, biográfico, anecdótico y legendario*, 134.

35. Heath Bowman and Stirling Dickinson, *Mexican Odyssey* (Chicago and New York: Willett, Clark and Co., 1935), 93.

36. Spratling, *File on Spratling*, 79.

37. Spratling's pieces were not pictured in the catalogue accompanying the exhibit, and they were deaccessioned in 1960. The museum has a pair of silver spurs made by Spratling for the prominent Algara family of Mexico, reproductions of colonial spurs used by an Algara ancestor. Kevin Stayton, curator of Decorative Arts, the Brooklyn Museum to author, July 6, 1995.

38. Elizabeth Anderson and Gerald Kelly, *Miss Elizabeth*, 241–42.

39. Interview with Mary Anita Loos von Saltza, May 15, 1995.

40. Interview with Gloria Castillo Gray, January 21, 1995.

41. Interview with Antonio Castillo, January 26, 1993; also, Spratling, *File on Spratling*, 195–96.

42. Penny C. Morrill, *Silver Masters of Mexico: Héctor Aguilar and the Taller Borda* (Atglen, Penn.: Schiffer Publishing Co., 1996), 38.

43. Ibid., 84.

44. Interview with anonymous Spratling friend, December 1993.

CHAPTER FIVE

1. Stromberg, *El juego del coyote,* 42.

2. Natalie Scott to Mrs. R. G. Robinson, May 23, 1938, Tulane University Archives.

3. Stromberg, *El Juego del Coyote,* 39; Spratling, *File on Spratling,* 7.

4. Interview with Castillo, January 26, 1993; Stromberg, *El juego del coyote,* 39, 42; Iturriaga, Prólogo to Spratling, *México tras lomita,* 1991, interview with Castillo, 53.

5. Spratling, *File on Spratling,* 61, 81.

6. William Spratling, "25 años de platería moderna," in *Artes de Mexico* 3, no. 10 (1955): 88.

7. Millicent Dillon, *A Little Original Sin: The Life and Work of Jane Bowles* (New York: Holt, Rinehart, and Winston, 1981), 88.

8. Ned Rorem, *Knowing When to Stop: A Memoir* (New York: Simon and Schuster, 1994), 147.

9. Elizabeth Anderson and Gerald R. Kelly, *Miss Elizabeth,* 252.

10. Ibid., 242.

11. Interview with Countess Gilberte Chartentenay, January 27, 1994.

12. The house is described by Paul Bowles in *Without Stopping: An Autobiography* (New York: Ecco Press, 1972), 227–28.

13. Interview with Carl Pappé, January 27, 1993.

14. Interview with Castillo; also 53, Castillo, Iturriaga, Prólogo to Spratling, *México tras lomita,* 53.

15. Mary Anita Loos, "Recuerdos de William Spratling," in *William Spratling Silver* (Mexico: Centro Cultural/Arte Contemporáneo, 1987), 20.

16. Interviews with Mary Anita Loos von Saltza, May 18, 1995; May 22, 1995.

17. Alba Guadalupe Mastache Flores and Elia Nora Morett Sánchez, *Entre dos mundo: Artesanos y artesanías en Guerrero* (Mexico: Instituto Nacional de Antropología e Historia, 1997), 208.

18. Interview with Countess Gilberte Chartentenay, January 27, 1994.

19. Moisés T. de la Peña, *Guerrero económico* (Mexico, 1949), quoted by Alba Guadalupe Mastache Flores and Elia Nora Morett Sánchez, *Entre dos mundos: Artesanos y artesanías en Guerrero* (Mexico: Instituto Nacional de Antropología e Historia, 1997), 207.

20. Spratling to Elizabeth Morrow, May 15, 1948, Spratling Ranch Archives; Penny Chittim Morrill and Carole A. Berk, *Mexican Silver,* 50–56. Spratling, *File on Spratling,* 119.

21. Interview with Antonio Castillo, January 26, 1993.

22. J. P. McEvoy, " 'Silver Bill,' Practical Good Neighbor," *Reader's Digest* 47 (September 1945): 19–22, 22.

23. Spratling, *File on Spratling,* 118–19.

24. McEvoy, "Silver Bill," 19.

CHAPTER SIX

1. Penny C. Morrill, *Silver Masters of Mexico: Hector Aguilar and the Taller Borda* (Atglen, Penn.: Schiffen Publishing Co., 1996), 186.

2. Robert David Duncan, "William Spratling's Mexican World," 97, 102.

3. Penny Chittim Morrill and Carole A. Berk, *Mexican Silver: 20th Century Handwrought Jewelry and Metalwork* (Atglen, Penn.: Schiffen Publishing Co., 1994), 143.

4. Ibid., 62–63.

5. Spratling to Lucille, October 11, 1949, Spratling Ranch Archives.

6. Interview with Margaret Donaghey, January 7, 1994.

7. Spratling, *File on Spratling,* 110–11.

8. Interview with Carl Pappé, January 27, 1993.

9. Janet Mandelstam, "Every Taxco cloud has a silver lining,*" The News* (February 12, 1965), Spratling Ranch Archives.

10. Ed Bleier to Spratling, n.d. but January 1947, Spratling Ranch Archives.

11. William Spratling, "Augustín Lorenzo, heroe de los juegos carnavalescos," *Mexican Folkways* 8, no. 1 (1933): 36–45.

12. Anon., "He's Teaching Eskimos in Mexico," *Times Picayune New States Orleans* magazine (June 5, 1949).

13. Spratling to Morrow, May 15, 1948, E. Morrow to Spratling, January 13, 1948, Spratling Ranch Archives.

14. Spratling to E. Morrow, November 19, 1949, Spratling Ranch Archives.

15. Clipping, *The Daily Alaskan,* n.d., Juneau, Spratling Ranch Archive.

16. This account of his trip is taken from "Flight to the North Star," *Flying* 46, no. 3 (March 1950):32–33, 51–52.

17. Penny Morrill and Carole A. Berk, *Mexican Silver,* 63.

18. Spratling, "Flight to the North Star," *Flying,* 51

19. Penny Morrill and Carole A. Berk, *Mexican Silver,* 64.

20. Interview with Margaret Donaghey, January 7, 1994.

21. Spratling, *File on Spratling,* 139.

22. Interview with Antonio Castillo, January 1993

23. Francis Eben to newspaper, January 11, 1949, Alaska Territorial Governor's Records (Series 130, Box 462, Files 462–66), National Archives. Also H. Allen Smith, *The Pig in the Barber Shop* (Boston: Little, Brown, 1958), 155.

24. Spratling, *File on Spratling,* 140.

25. Ibid., 129; also Penny Morrill and Carole A. Berk, *Mexican Silver,* 66.

26. Morrill and Carole A. Berk., *Mexican Silver,* 66.

27. Mary L. Davis and Greta Pack, *Mexican Jewelry* (Austin: University of Texas Press, 1963), 176, 179.

28. All information on Puiforcat is from Françoise de Bonneville, *Puiforcat* (Paris: Editions du Regard, 1986).

29. Spratling, *File on Spratling,* 81.

30. Spratling, "25 Years of Modern Silver," *Artes de México* 3, no. 10 (1955): 88–89.

31. Ibid., 89.

32. Spratling, "The True Color of Silver is White," *Mexico This Month* 2, no. 6 (1956): 13.

33. Interview with John Stokes, December 14, 1993.

34. Telephone interview with Stanley Marcus, June 28, 1995.

35. Interview with Emilia Castillo, January 20, 1994.

36. Natalie Scott to Martha Gilmore Robinson, December 30, 1951, Tulane University Archives.

37. Mary Daniels, clipping, "The Many Sides of William Spratling," no other information.

38. Spratling, *File on Spratling,* 202–4. The date was December 30, 1952, from the *New York Times* announcement of Nancy Oakes's marriage, 17.

39. Natalie Scott to M. G. Robinson, March 29, 1953, Tulane University Archives.

40. H. Allen Smith, *The Pig in the Barber Shop,* 151, 161; population and tourist impact from Erna Fergusson, *Mexico Revisited* (New York: Knopf, 1955), 246.

41. H. Allen Smith, ibid., 173.

42. Interview with Margaret Donaghey, January 7, 1994.

43. Interview with Carl Pappé, January 27, 1993.

44. Elizabeth Anderson and Gerald R. Kelly, *Miss Elizabeth: A Memoir* (Boston: Little, Brown and Co., 1969), 274.

45. Interview with Gerald R. Kelly, October 17, 1994; Margaret Donaghey, "A Creative American: Elizabeth Prall Anderson," VISTAS Section, *The News* [Mexico City] (December 8, 1974), clipping courtesy of Margaret Donaghey.

CHAPTER SEVEN

136   1. Quoted in Barbara Braun, "Diego Rivera's Collection: Pre-Columbian Art as Political and Artistic Legacy," in Elizabeth Hill Boone, ed., *Collecting the Pre-Columbian Past* (Washington, D.C.: Dumbarton Oaks Research Library and Collection, 1993), 251–70, 253.

2. Spratling, *File on Spratling,* 153.

3. Ibid., 175.

4. Spratling to Zigrosser, August 27, 1930, Carl Zigrosser Papers, Archives of American Art, Smithsonian Institution. On the early market, see Michael D. Coe, "From Huaquero to Connoisseur: The Early Market in Pre-Columbian Art," in Boone, *Collecting the Pre-Columbian Past,* 271–90.

5. Spratling to Carl Zigrosser, November 22, 1931, Carl Zigrosser Papers, Archives of American Art, Smithsonian Institution.

6. Spratling, *File on Spratling,* 188–90. Covarrubias made a drawing of the wooden mask and, with his greater concern for archaeological data, named the exact place from which it had come—a cave on the Cerro de la Cruz, Canón de la Mano, five kilometers from Iguala. (See Miguel Covarrubias, "La Venta: Colossal Heads and Jaguar Gods," *DYN* 6 (1944): 24–32.)

7. Clipping from *New Orleans Tribune,* n.d., in Spratling Scrapbook, Spratling Ranch Archives. Zigrosser to Franz Blom, November 1, 1938, Carl Zigrosser Papers, Archives of America Art, Smithsonian Institution.

8. Interview with Carl Pappé, January 27, 1993.

9. Telephone interview with Jaime Castrejón, April 19, 1992.

10. Michael Coe, "From Huaquero to Connoisseur: The Early Market in Pre-Columbian Art," 284.

11. Daniel F. Rubín de la Borbolla, "William Spratling, Pionero," in *William Spratling* (Mexico: Centro cultural/Arte Contemporáneo, A.C., 1987), 15.

12. Telephone interview with Jaime Castrejón, April 19, 1992, who was told the story by Spratling.

13. Miguel Covarrubias, "Tlatilco, Archaic Mexican Art and Culture," *DYN: The Review of Modern Art* 4–5 (1943): 40–46, 41.

14. Miguel Covarrubias, "Tlatilco: El arte y la cultura preclásica del Valle de México," *Cuadernos Americanos* 60, no. 3 (May-June 1950), 153.

15. Spratling made three sets of photostats of his collection of clay seals. He sent one to Franz Blom at Tulane and another to Herbert Spinden, Latin American Library, Tulane University.

16. Covarrubias, *DYN* (1943): 45.

17. Adriana Williams, *Covarrubias* (Austin: University of Texas Press, 1994), 14;
    also Covarrubias, "Tlatilco: El arte y la culture preclásica del Valle de
    México," 151.

18. Adriana Williams, *Covarrubias,* 144.

19. Interview with Margareta González Banda, January 21, 1992.

20. Miguel Covarrubias, *Indian Art of Mexico and Central America* (New York:
    Knopf, 1957), 53.

21. Miguel Covarrubias, "Tipologia de la industria de piedra tallada y pulida de
    la cuenca del Rio Mezcala," *Sociedad Mexicana de Antropología,* 4th
    Reunión de Mesa Redondo (1946): 86–90.

22. Gillett G. Griffin, "Formative Guerrero and its Jade," in Frederick W.
    Lange, ed., *Pre-Columbian Jade* (Salt Lake City: University of Utah Press,
    1993), 203–10, 207. Also Carlo Gay, *Mexcala Architecture in Miniature*
    (Brussels: Academie Royale de Belgique, 1987), and Carlo Gay, *Guerrero
    Stone Sculpture from the Luis de Hoyos Collection* (South Fallsburg, N.Y.:
    Sullivan County Community College, 1965).

23. Spratling, *File on Spratling,* 176.

24. Ibid., 178, 183.

25. Rafael Ruiz Harrell, "Sombras de un naufragio," in Efrán Castro, Carlo
    T. E. Gay, Eduardo Matos Moctezuma, Bertina Olmedo, Rafael Parres,
    Rafael Ruiz Harrell, Jacqueline Sáenz, Mari Carmen Serra Puche, Manuel
    de la Torre, Javier Wimer, *El arte de Mezcala* (Mexico: Espejo de Obsidiana,
    1993), 34.

26. Jacqueline Sáenz, "Un remoto ante moderno," in ibid., 99, author's
    translation. The Sáenz Collection was installed in the early 1990s in the
    Museo Amparo in Puebla. The Leof-Brenman Collection in the mid-1990s
    still in the possession of Brenman's widow, Nadine Vinot, may become the
    nucleus of a museum in Acapulco.

27. William Spratling, "More Human Than Divine," in *More Human Than
    Divine* (Mexico: Universidad Nacional Autónoma de México, 1964), 16. Ted
    J. J. Leyenaar, Gerard W. van Bussel, and Gesine Weber, *From Coast to
    Coast: Precolumbian Sculpture from Meso-America* (Kassel and Leiden, 1992),
    124ff.

28. Jose Iturriaga, Prólogo to William Spratling, *México tras lomita* (Mexico:
    Editorial Diana, 1991), interview with Josué Sáenz, 49. Rosa Covarrubias
    was not much more fond of him. In 1959 when she was suing the National
    Museum of Anthropology in Mexico over their dispersal of the vast
    collection Covarrubias had given them (some 976 pieces), she wrote to

Nelson Rockefeller: "When we win a point and are about to move forward Mr. Spratling's lawyer is there to stop us on some stupid technical point. I really don't know what to do about him. He is in Mexico by the skin of his teeth anyhow. . . . " Quoted by Adriana Williams in *Covarrubias,* 237, from Nelson A. Rockefeller Collection, Series Countries, Sub-series Mexico. Box 52, folder 433, Rockefeller Family Archive, Rockefeller Archive Center.

29. Spratling, *File on Spratling,* 156.

30. The book on jade, which was to be co-authored by Thomas G. Clements, professor of geology at the University of Southern California and curator at the Los Angeles County Museum, was never finished.

31. James F. Garber, David C. Grove, Kenneth C. Hirth, and John W. Hoopes, "Jade Use in Portions of Mexico and Central America," in F. Lange, *Pre-Columbian Jade,,* 211–31, 212.

32. Frederick A. Peterson, "Falsificaciones arqueológicas en el Estado de Guerrero, México," *Tlatoani, Boletin de la Sociedad de alumnos de la Escuela nacional de antropología e historia* 1, nos. 3 and 4 (August 1952): 15–19; also Frederick A. Peterson, "Faces that are really false," *Natural History* 62, no. 4 (April 1953): 176–80.

33. Peterson, "Falsificaciones arqueológicas," in *Tlatoani,* 18.

34. Interview with Ezekiel Tapia, 1994. Also Penny Morrill, *Mexican Silver,* 212–13.

35. Interview with Antonio Castillo, January 19, 1992.

36. Interview with John Stokes, December 14, 1993.

37. Interview with Margaret Donaghey, January 7, 1994.

38. Spratling to Tatiana Proskouriakoff, April 23, 1960, letter courtesy of Shawn Erik Simpson.

39. Tatiana Proskouriakoff diaries, April 6, 1960, Harvard University Archives.

40. Tatiana Proskouriakoff diaries, January 2, 1960, Harvard University Archives.

41. Josué Sáenz, in Iturriaga, ed., Prólogo to William Spratling, *Mexico tras lomita,,* 39.

42. Quoted by Alberto Ruy-Sanchez Lacy in "A Labyrinth of Echoes," trans. by Roberto Tejada, *Artes de México* 28 (1995): 73, "La falsificación y sus espejos."

43. Telephone interview with Anne Clements Eldred, May 1995.

44. René d'Harnoncourt to Nelson Rockefeller, June 10, 1959, folder 1652, box 162, Project Series Nelson A. Rockefeller, Personal, Rockefeller Family Archive, Rockefeller Archive Center, Pocantico Hills, Sleepy Hollow, New York.

45. Nelson Rockefeller to Philip F. Kebler, July 24, 1957; Robert Goldwater to Nelson Rockefeller, May 7, 1957, ibid. [folder 1652, box 162].

46. Spratling to René d'Harnoncourt, n.d. but included in letter d'Harnoncourt to Nelson Rockefeller, August 6, 1959, ibid. [folder 1652, box 162].

47. Robert Goldwater to Nelson Rockefeller, October 30, 1959, and note added at top, dated 11/14/59., ibid.

48. Interview with Carl Pappé, January 27, 1993.

139

CHAPTER EIGHT

1. Interview with Mary Anita Loos von Saltza, May 18, 1995.

2. Telephone interview with David Read, June 5, 1998.

3. Helen Escobedo in Iturriaga, Prólogo to William Spratling, *México tras lomita,* 70.

4. Budd Schulberg, Introduction to Spratling, *File on Spratling,* xiii. Spratling's daily schedule at the ranch is from Gerald R. Kelly, "William Spratling: Arquitecto-diseñador," in *William Spratling* (Mexico: Centro Cultural/Arte Contemporáneo, 1987), 30–31.

5. Ibid.

6. Ibid., xi.

7. Spratling, *File on Spratling,* 220–30.

8. Interview with Deva Garro, April 22, 1992.

9. Interview with Antonio Castillo, January 19, 1992.

10. Interview with Antonio Pineda, January 22, 1994.

11. Interview with Antonio Castillo, January 19, 1992.

12. Card and reprint courtesy of Ian Graham. The article is "The William Spratling Collection," *The Architectural Digest* 22, no. 3 (Winter 1965): 90–95.

13. Telephone interview with Stanley Marcus, June 28, 1995. The strawberry incident is also in Spratling, *File on Spratling,* 229–30.

14. Eunice Murray with Rose Shade, *Marilyn: The Last Months* (New York: Pyramid Books, 1975), 62.

15. Spratling, *File on Spratling,* 211–16.

16. Interview with Margareta González Banda; also in Iturriaga, Prólogo, 64–67.

17. Henry Seldin, "William Spratling, All that Glitters is not Gold," *Los Angeles Times* (September 10, 1965), clipping in Spratling Ranch Archives.

18. Booklet on the reception is in the Rockefeller Family Archive.

19. "The World of William Spratling," exhibit catalogue, Rockefeller Family Archive.

20. Interview with Ted Wick, January 17, 1992.

21. Interview with Gerald R. Kelly, October 17, 1994.

22. Dewey Wayne Gunn, *American and British Writers in Mexico, 1556–1973* (Austin: University of Texas Press, 1974), 149.

140   23. Spratling to Tatiana Proskouriakoff, December 12, 1966, Shawn Erik Simpson collection.

24. According to Luis Aveleyra de Anda, *Obras selectas del arte prehispánico* (Mexico: Museo Nacional de Antropología, 1964) Spratling gave the National Museum of Anthropology 26 Mixtec and Teotihuacan vessels and sold or exchanged or gave in lieu of some other obligation 102 other pieces.

25. Interview with Margarita González Banda. The date of the prostate operation is from Spratling to Caroline Durieux, May 13, 1967, Caroline Durieux Papers, Archives of American Art, Smithsonian Institution.

26. Interview with Ted Wick, January 17, 1992.

27. Interview with Jaime Castrejón, April 30, 1992. A museum was built in Taxco to house Spratling's archaeological collection. Experts familiar with what Spratling had at the ranch insist however that the two collections are not the same. Considerable slippage or theft occurred between the time of Spratling's death and the eventual installation of the collection in the new museum building. The collection is riddled with fakes, some now labeled "reproduction."

28. Anderson and Kelly, *Miss Elizabeth,* 296.

29. José Vasconcelos and Manuel Gamio, *Aspects of Mexican Civilization* (Chicago: University of Chicago Press, 1926), 27.

30. Josué Sáenz, in Iturriaga, Prólogo to William Spratling, *México tras lomita,* 47.

31. Interview with Ted Wick, January 17, 1992.

32. *The News* (August 20, 1967): 11b–13b.

33. Interview with Gerald R. Kelly, October 17, 1994.

34. Elizabeth Anderson to Caroline Durieux, September 10, 1967, and Anderson to Durieux, n.d., but several weeks later, Caroline Durieux Papers, Archives of American Art, Smithsonian Institution.

35. The entire speech was printed in one of the Taxco papers, August 1967, clipping from private collection.

36. Interview with Teresa Domínguez Islas and Efrim Domínguez, January 1996.

BIBLIOGRAPHY

WORKS BY WILLIAM SPRATLING:

William Spratling. *Pencil Drawing,* illustrated by the author. New Orleans: The Penguin Book Shop, 1923.

——. *Picturesque New Orleans.* Ten drawings of the French Quarter with introduction by Lyle Saxon. Rev. ed. New Orleans: Tulane University Press, 1923.

——. *Sherwood Anderson and Other Famous Creoles.* Introduction by William Faulkner. New Orleans: Pelican Bookshop Press, 1926. Reprinted in *The Texas Quarterly* 9 (Spring 1966).

——. "Old Plantation Architecture in Louisiana." Part 1: "The Early Period, and Houses of the Bayou Country" and Part 2: "The Result of French and Spanish Influence," *The Architectural Forum* 44, no. 4 (April 1926): 216–44 and 44, no. 5 (May 1926): 301–6.

——, with Natalie Scott. *Old Plantation Houses in Louisiana.* New York: William Helbrun, 1927.

——. "Natchez, Mississippi." *Architectural Forum* 49 (November 1927): 425–28.

——. "The Architectural Heritage of New Orleans." *Architectural Forum* 46, no. 5 (May 1927): 409–13.

——. "Some Impressions of Mexico," 2 parts. *Architectural Forum* 47, no. 1 (July 1927): 1–8 and no. 2 (August 1927): 161–68.

——. "Cane River Portraits." *Scribner's Magazine* 83 (April 1928): 411–18.

——. "Guanajuato, the Most Mexican City." *Architectural Forum* 48 (February 1928): 217–22.

——. "Indo-Hispanic Mexico," 2 parts. *Architecture* (February 1929): 75–80; (March 1929): 139–44.

——. "Figures in a Mexican Renaissance." *Scribner's Magazine* 85 (January 1929): 14–20.

——. "The Silver City of the Clouds." *Travel* 53, no. 3 (July 1929): 22–23.

———. "Mansions of the Conquistadors." *Travel* 53, no. 4 (August 1929): 28–31.

———. "Friendly Capital of Rebel Mexico." *Travel* 53, no. 5 (September 1929):

142   35–36

———. "Mexican Letter." *Sunday New York Herald Tribune,* Books Section (March 24, 1929): 11; also "Orozco" (April 14, 1929): 11; "Re-Creating a University" (June 2, 1929): 9; "Review of Jacques Lacretelle, *Marie Bonifas*" (June 2, 1929): 16; "Mexican Letter" (July 28, 1929): 9; "Mexican Letter" (November 10, 1929): 9; "Mexican Letter" (January 29, 1930): 9; "The Arts and Letters in Mexico" (June 8, 1930): 9; "Votes for Mexico"(December 7, 1930): 9; "Literary Notes from Mexico" (March 8, 1931): 9; "Mexican Letter" (July 5, 1931): 9, all in Books Section, *Sunday New York Herald Tribune.*

———. "The Frescoes of Diego Rivera." *Mexican Folk-Ways* 5, no. 4 (1929): 205.

———. "Diego Rivera." *Mexican Folk-Ways* 6, no. 4 (1930): 162–73.

———, ed. *The Frescoes of Diego Rivera.* New York: Museum of Modern Art, 1930.

———. *Siqueiros: 13 Woodcuts.* N.p., 1931.

———., "Some New Discoveries in Mexican Clay." *International Studio* 98 (February 1931): 22–23.

———. *Little Mexico.* New York: Jonathan Cape and Harrison Smith, 1932. Reprinted as *A Small Mexican World.* Boston: Little, Brown, 1964. Spanish edition, *México tras lomita,* trans. by Fernando Horcasitas. Mexico: Editorial Diana, 1965. New edition, *México tras lomita,* with Prologo by José N. Iturriaga, including interviews with eleven people who knew Spratling. Mexico: Editorial Diana, 1991.

———. "Augustin Lorenzo." *Mexican Folk-Ways* 8 no. 1 (January-March 1933): 36–45.

———. "Modern Mexican Silversmithing." *Mexican Art and Life* 3 (July 1937), reprinted as "Platería mexicana moderna," in *William Spratling.* Mexico: Centro Cultural/Arte Contemporáneo, 1987, 35–38.

———. *Fine Mexican Silver by Spratling.* Catalogue and price list, Taxco, 1944.

———. "Flight to the North Star." *Flying* 46 (March 1950): 32–33.

———. "25 Años de Platería Moderna." *Artes de México* 3, no. 10 (1955): 87–90.

———. "The True Color of Silver Is White." *Mexico This Month* 2, no. 6 (1956): 13ff.

———. "Notes," in Miguel Covarrubias, *Mexcala: Ancient Mexican Sculpture.* New York: André Emmerich Gallery, 1956.

———. *Más humano que divino.* Preface by Gordon Eckholm; archaeological note by Alfonso Medellin Zenil; photos by Manuel Alvarez Bravo. Mexico: Universidad Nacional Autónoma de México, 1960.

———. "Notes on the Pre-Columbian Sculpture of Guerrero," in Daniel F. R. de la Borbolla, *Escultura precolombina de Guerrero.* Mexico: Universidad Nacional Autónoma de México, 1964.

———. "Chronicle of a Friendship: William Faulkner in New Orleans." *The Texas Quarterly* 9 (Spring 1966): 34–40.

———. *File on Spratling: An Autobiography.* Boston: Little, Brown, 1967.

———. "El renacimiento de Taxco (por un tasqueño nacido en Nueva York)." *Revista de la Universidad de México* 23, no. 11 (July 1968).

———. *William Spratling Design Portfolio.* Mexico: Centro Cultural/Arte Contemporáneo, 1987,

N. C. Curtin, and William Spratling. *The Wrought Iron Work of Old New Orleans.* New York: Press of the American Institute of Architects, 1925.

OTHER WORKS:

Anderson, Elizabeth, and Gerald R. Kelly. *Miss Elizabeth: A Memoir.* Boston: Little, Brown, 1969.

Anderson, Lawrence. *The Art of the Silversmith in Mexico, 1519–1936,* 2 vols. New York: Oxford University Press, 1941.

Anderson, Sherwood. *Southern Odyssey: Selected Writings by,* edited by Welford Dunaway Taylor and Charles E. Modlin. Athens: University of Georgia Press, 1997.

Beals, Carleton. *The Great Circle: Further Adventures in Free-Lancing.* Philadelphia: J. B. Lippincott, 1940.

Benjamin, R. S. "Eskimos Down South." *Americas* 1 (September 1949): 26–27.

Blotner, Joseph. *Faulkner, a Biography.* New York: Random House, 1974.

de Bonneville, Françoise. *Jean Puiforcat.* Paris: Editions du Regard, 1986.

Boone, Elizabeth Hill, ed. *The Aztec Templo Mayor.* Washington, D.C.: Dumbarton Oaks, 1987.

———, ed. *Collecting the Pre-Columbian Past.* Washington, D.C.: Dumbarton Oaks, 1993.

Bowen, Frances Jean. "The New Orleans Double Dealer, 1921–1926." *The Louisiana Historical Quarterly* 39 (October 1956): 443–56.

Bowles, Paul. *Without Stopping: An Autobiography.* New York: Ecco Press, 1972.

Bowman, Heath, and Stirling Dickinson. *Mexican Odyssey.* Chicago: Willet, Clark, 1935.

Brading, D. A., and Harry E. Cross. "Colonial Silver Mining: Mexico and Peru." *Hispanic American Historical Review* 52 (1972): 545–79.

Brenner, Anita. *Idols Behind Altars.* New York: Harcourt Brace, 1929.

Brown, Susan Jenkins. *Robber Rocks: Letters and Memories of Hart Crane, 1923–1932.* Middletown, Conn.: Wesleyan University Press, 1969.

Castrejón, Jaime Díez. "Taxco and Its Origins" *Artes de México* 5 (Fall 1989): 82–85.

———, and Ruby N. Castrejón. *William Spratling.* Taxco: 1968.

Castro, Efrán, Carlo T. W. Gay, Eduardo Matos Moctezuma, Bertina Olmedo, Rafael Parres, Rafael Ruiz Harrell, Jacqueline Sáenz, Mari Carmen Serra Puche, Manuel de la Torre, Javier Wimer. *El arte de Mezcala.* Mexico: Espejo de Obsidiana, 1993.

Cederwall, Sandraline, and Hal Riney, with Barnaby Conrad. *Spratling Silver.* San Francisco: Chronicle Books, 1990.

Chase, Stuart. *Mexico: A Study of Two Americas.* New York: Macmillan, 1931.

Collier, C. Kirby. "History of the Section on Convulsive Disorder and Related Efforts." *The American Journal of Psychiatry* 101 (1944–45): 468–71.

Cordry, Donald. *Mexican Masks.* Foreword by Peter T. Furst. Austin: University of Texas Press, 1980.

———, and Dorothy Cordry. *Mexican Indian Costumes.* Austin: University of Texas Press, 1968.

Covarrubias, Miguel. "Notas sobre máscaras mexicanas." *Mexican Folk-Ways* 5, no. 3 (1929).

———. "Tlatilco: Archaic Mexican Art and Culture" *DYN: The Review of Modern Art* 4–5 (1943): 40–46.

———. "La Venta: Colossal Heads and Jaguar Gods." *DYN: The Review of Modern Art* 6 (1944): 24–32.

———. "Tipologia de la industria de piedra tallada y pulida de la cuenca del Rio Mezcala." *Sociedad Mexicana de Antropología, 4th Reunión de Mesa Redondo* (1946): 86–90.

———. "Tlatilco, El arte y la cultura preclásica del Valle de México." *Cuadernos Americanos* 60, no. 3 (May-June, 1950): 153.

———. *Indian Art of Mexico and Central America.* New York: Knopf, 1957.

Cox, Beverly J., and Deana Jones Anderson. *Miguel Covarrubias: Caricatures.* Washington, D.C.: National Portrait Gallery, 1985.

Contemporary Industrial and Handwrought Silver. Exhibit catalogue. Brooklyn, N.Y.: Brooklyn Museum, 1937.

Davis, Mary, and Greta Pack. *Mexican Jewelry.* Austin: University of Texas Press, 1963.

Day, Michael. "Mexico's City of Silver." *Popular Mechanics* 97 (June 1952): 120–24.

Delpar, Helen. *The Enormous Vogue of Things Mexican: Cultural Relations*

Between the United States and Mexico, 1920–1935. Tuscaloosa: University of Alabama Press, 1992.

Díaz Oyarzábal, Clara Luz. *Colección de objetos de piedra, obsidiana, concha, metales y textiles del Estado de Guerrero.* Mexico: Instituto Nacional de Antropología e Historia, 1990.

Dillon, Millicent. *A Little Original Sin: The Life and Work of Jane Bowles.* New York: Holt, Rinehart, and Winston, 1981.

Domínguez Islas, Margarita. *Taxco histórico, biográfico, anecdótico y legendario.* Acapulco: privately printed, 1980.

Duncan, Robert David. "William Spratling's Mexican World." *Texas Quarterly* 9 (Spring 1966): 97–104.

Easby, Elizabeth Kennedy, and John E. Scott. *Before Cortés: Sculpture of Middle America.* New York: Metropolitan Museum of Art, 1970.

Eckholm, Gordon F. "The Problem of Fakes in Pre-Columbian Art." *Curator* 7, no. 1 (1964): 19–32.

Eshelman, Catharine Good. *Hacienda La Lucha: Arte y comercio nahuas de Guerrero.* Mexico: Fondo de Cultura Económica, 1988.

"La falsificación y sus espejos." *Artes de México* 28 (1995).

Fergusson, Erna. *Mexico Revisited.* New York: Knopf, 1955.

"Fiesta at Taxco: Silver Crafts and Bill Spratling." *Time* 38, no. 1 (July 7, 1941): 26.

Faulkner, William. *Mosquitoes.* New York: Liveright, 1955 (orig., 1927).

———. *William Faulkner: New Orleans Sketches,* edited by Carvel Collins. New York: Random House, 1968.

———. *Soldiers' Pay.* New York: Boni and Liveright, 1926.

Figueroa, Leslie C. de. *Taxco: The Enchanted Hill-town: A Handbook for Tourists.* Taxco, Guerrero: privately printed, 1960, rev. ed., 1965.

———. *Stuffed Shirt in Taxco.* Taxco, Guerrero: Taxco School of Art, 1961.

Foscue, Edwin J. *Taxco: Mexico's Silver City.* Dallas: Southern Methodist University Press, 1947.

Furst, Peter T. "West Mexican Art: Secular or Sacred?" In *Iconography of Middle American Sculpture.* New York: Metropolitan Museum of Art, 1973.

García-Noriega Nieto, Lucia. "Mexican Silver: William Spratling and the Taxco Style." *Journal of Decorative and Propaganda Arts* 10 (Fall 1988): 42–53.

Gay, Carlo. *Guerrero Stone Sculpture from the Luis de Hoyos Collection.* South Fallsburg, N.Y.: Sullivan County Community College, 1965.

———. *Mezcala Architecture in Miniature.* Brussels: Academie Royale de Belgique, 1987.

Gunn, Dewey Wayne. *American and British Writers in Mexico, 1556–1973.* Austin: University of Texas Press, 1974.

Hellman, Geoffray T. "Imperturbable noble" [René d'Harnoncourt] *The New Yorker* (May 7, 1960): 49, 112.

146   Holditch, W. Kenneth. "William Faulkner, William Spratling, and Other Famous Creoles." Unpublished ms., courtesy of the author.

Huxley, Aldous. *Beyond the Mexique Bay.* New York and London: Harper, 1934.

Jelliffe, Smith Ely. "William P. Spratling." *Journal of Nervous and Mental Diseases* 45 (1917): 191–92.

Karl, Frederick R. *William Faulkner: American Writer.* New York: Ballantine, 1989.

La Farge, Oliver. *Raw Material.* Boston: Houghton Mifflin, 1945.

Lange, Frederick W., ed.. *Pre-Columbian Jade: New Geological and Cultural Interpretations.* Salt Lake City: University of Utah Press, 1993.

Leyenaar, Ted J., Gerard W. Van Bussel, and Gesine Weber. *From Coast to Coast: Pre-Columbian Sculpture from Meso-America.* Kassel and Leiden: Weber and Weidemeyer, 1992.

McEvoy, J. P. " 'Silver Bill,' Practical Good Neighbor" *Reader's Digest* 47 (September 1945): 19–22.

Mandelstam, Janet. "Every Taxco Cloud Has a Silver Lining," *The News* [Mexico City] (February 12, 1965).

Mastache Flores, Alba Guadalupe, and Elia Nora Morett Sánchez. *Entre dos mundo: Artesanos y artesanías en Guerrero.* Mexico: Instituto Nacional de Antropología e Historia, 1997.

Medina, Andrés. "Miguel Covarrubias y el romanticismo en la antropología." *Nueva Antropologiá* [Mexic]o (1976): 11–41.

Morrill, Penny Chittim. *Hecho en Mexico.* Bethesda, Md.: Carole A. Berk, 1990.

———, and Carole A. Berk. *Mexican Silver: 20th Century Handwrought Jewelry and Metalwork.* Atglen, Penn.: Schiffer, 1994.

———. *Silver Masters of Mexico: Héctor Aguilar and the Taller Borda.* Atglen, Penn.: Schiffer, 1996.

Morrow, Elizabeth. *Casa Mañana,* with drawings by William Spratling. Privately printed, 1937.

———. *The Mexican Years.* New York: Spiral Press, 1953.

Murray, Eunice, with Rose Shade. *Marilyn: The Last Months.* New York: Pyramid, 1975.

"Obituary: William P. Spratling of Welaka." *Journal of the Florida Medical Society* 1 (1915).

Oles, James. *South of the Border: Mexico in the American Imagination, 1914–1947.* Washington, D.C.: Smithsonian Institution Press, 1993.

Pantel, Harold James, and Arthur Daniel Pomroy. *A History of Craig Colony with 50 Years of the Colonists' Club.* N.p., n.d.

Peterson, Frederick A. "Falsificaciones arqueologicas en el Estado de Guerrero, Mexico." *Tlatoani* [Boletín de la Sociedad de Alumnos de la Escuela Nacional de antropologia y historia] 1, nos. 3–4 (August 1952): 15–19.

———. "Faces That Are Really False." *Natural History* 62, no. 4 (April 1953), 176–80.

Proskouriakoff, Tatiana. Review of *More Human Than Divine. American Antiquity* 27, no. 3 (1962): 439.

Rojado Ojeda, Vladimir. "El oro y la plata en el México antiguo." *Artes de México* 3, no. 10 (1955):5–24.

Romero, Christie. "William Spratling and the Taxco School." *Heritage: Jewelers' Circular-Keystone* (March 1993): 68–75.

Rorem, Ned. *Knowing When To Stop: A Memoir.* New York: Simon and Schuster, 1994.

Schmidt, Henry C. "The American Intellectual Discovery of Mexico in the 1920s." *South Atlantic Quarterly* 77 (1978): 335–51.

Scott, Natalie. "Peggy Passe Partout." *New Orleans States,* c. 1925–29, columns, in Natalie Scott Papers, Special Collections, Tulane University Library.

———. "Don Guillermo of Taxco." *The New Orleanian* (November 15, 1930):16–17, 30.

Smith, H. Allen. *The Pig in the Barber Shop.* Boston: Little, Brown, 1958.

Spratling, William P. [Sr.] *The Craig Colony for Epileptics at Sonyea, in Livingston County, New York; Bulletin of General Information.* Buffalo: Matthews Northrup, 1902.

———. *Epilepsy and Its Treatment.* Philadelphia and London: W. B. Saunders, 1904.

Stromberg, Gobi. *El juego del coyote: Platería y arte en Taxco.* Mexico: Fondo de Cultura Económica, 1985.

Tibol, Raquel. "David Alfaro Siqueiros en Taxco." *Artes de México* 5 (Fall 1989): 92–95.

Tibón, Gutierre. *El jade de México.* Mexico: Panorama Editorial, 1983.

Toussaint, Manuel. *Tasco,* illustrated by William Spratling. Mexico: Publicaciones de la secretaria de Hacienda, 1931.

———. *Oaxaca y Taxco.* Lectures 80 Mexicanas. Mexico: Fondo de Cultura Económica, 1967.

Townsend, Kim. *Sherwood Anderson.* Boston: Houghton Mifflin, 1987.

Vasconcelos, José, and Manuel Gamio. *Aspects of Mexican Civilization.* Chicago: University of Chicago Press, 1926.

Walsh, Thomas F. *Katherine Anne Porter and Mexico: The Illusion of Eden.* Austin: University of Texas Press, 1992.

147

Watson, James G., ed. *Thinking of Home: William Faulkner's Letters to His Mother and Father, 1918–1925.* New York: Norton, 1992.

148   Weber, Brom, ed. *The Letters of Hart Crane, 1916–1932.* New York: Hermitage House, 1952.

"The William Spratling Collection" [photos of Spratling's house museum]. *Architectural Digest* 22, no. 3 (Winter 1965): 90–95.

William Spratling. Exhibit catalogue, ed. by Lucia García Noriega Nieto, with essays by Daniel F. Rubín de la Borbolla, Mary Anita Loos, Gerald R. Kelly, and Spratling. Mexico: Centro Cultural/Arte Contemporáneo, 1987.

Williams, Adriana. *Covarrubias.* Austin: University of Texas Press, 1994.

Acknowledgments

This book could not have been written without the help of a great many people. I am particularly grateful to Alberto M. Ulrich of William Spratling Sucesores, S.A., in Taxco, for his hospitality and enthusiastic cooperation, and to Mary Anita Loos von Saltza and her husband Carl von Saltza, for her willingness to be interviewed at length and the pleasure of their company in Santa Monica.

The many others who were unfailingly generous with their time and knowledge include: Enrique and Peggy Alferez, Manuel Alvarez Bravo, Antonio Castillo, Emilia Castillo, Gloria Castillo Gray, Javier Castillo, María de los Angeles G. de Castillo, Jaime Castrejón Diez, Thomas Clements, Salvador G. De Velasco Domínguez, Efrim Domínguez, Teresa Domínguez Islas, Margaret Donaghey, Ann Clements Eldred, André Emmerich, Helen Escobedo, Juan Estrada, Beatrice Fuchs, Deva Garro, Carlo Gay, Phyllis Goddard, Charles Goff, Hector Gómez Villalobos, Margarita González Banda, Ian Graham, Gillett Griffin, W. Kenneth Holditch, Wendy Jimenez, Bertin Juarez, Gerald R. Kelly, Frederick W. Lange, Jalil Majul Ballesteros, Carlos Manning, Stanley Marcus, Susan N. Masuoka, Gabriel Medina Williams, Andrés Mejia Alvarez, Juan Jose Melendez, Penny C. Morrill, Padre Efrén Neri Rondón, Lucia Noriega-Garcia y Nieto, James Oles, Dolores Olmedo Patiño, Carl Pappé, Ross Parmenter, Antonio Pineda, Sigi Pineda, Manuel Quinto, David Read, Luis Reyes Ramirez, Manolo Sandoval, John W. Scott, Shawn Erik Simpson, Sally Sloan, Alfonso Soto Soria, John Stokes, Gobi Stromberg, Ezekiel Tápia, Gutierre Tibón, Tomás Vega, Ted Wick, Adriana Williams.

I would like to thank the following archivists and curators who answered queries and provided materials: Agustin Avila Ramirez, Museum of the National University of Mexico; Clara Luz Díaz Oyarzábal, National Anthropology Museum; Susan L. Boone, curator, Sophia Smith Collection, Smith College; Melissa B. Falkner, registrar, Birmingham Museum of Art; Beatrice Fuchs, Spratling Ranch; Gillett Griffin, The Art Museum, Princeton University; Harvey B. Gross, Craig Developmental Disabilities Service Office, Geneseo, New York; Jinger

Heffner, coordinator, Otis College of Art and Design, Los Angeles; Harold W. Oakhill, archivist, Rockefeller Family Archive; Courtney Page, Special Collections, Tulane University Library; José Juárez Sánche, Fundación Dolores Olmedo; Joanne Sealy and Joe de Salvo at Faulkner House Books, New Orleans; Kevin Stayron, curator, Department of Decorative Arts, The Brooklyn Museum; Loa Traxler, assistant curator, Dumbarton Oaks; Dieter C. Ullrich, coordinator, Paul Meek Library, The University of Tennessee.

I have used the William Spratling Papers at the William Spratling Ranch, Taxco, Guerrero, Mexico; William Spratling files, New Orleans Historical Collection; Caroline Durieux Papers, René d'Harnoncourt Papers, and Carl Zigrosser Papers at the Archives of American Art, Smithsonian Institution; Record Group 4, Nelson A. Rockefeller-Personal, Countries Series and Projects Series Papers, Rockefeller Archive Center, Sleepy Hollow, New York; Elizabeth Morrow Papers at Smith College; Martha Robinson Papers, Lyle Saxon Papers, and Natalie Scott Papers, Tulane University; Latin American Library Collection, Tulane University; Tatiana Proskouriakoff Papers, Harvard University Archives; Holland McCombs Papers at the Paul Meek Library, University of Tennessee; Records of the Indian Arts and Crafts Board relating to arts and crafts projects in Alaska (RG 435, Box 7) National Archives; Alaska Territorial Governor's Records (Series 130, Box 462, File 462–6) National Archives.

INDEX